THE CEO
GOES TO
WASHINGTON

ALSO BY

Max Holland

◆

When the Machine Stopped:
A Cautionary Tale From
Industrial America

the chief executive press

THE CEO GOES TO WASHINGTON

MAX HOLLAND

whittle direct books

Photographs: John A. Young by Ed Kashi, page 9;
Rene Anselmo by Rob Kinmonth, page 27; Henry R. Kravis
by Jonathan Levine, page 45; William T. McCormick Jr.
by Paul Elledge, page 63.
Illustration by Neal Walker, page 37.

The Chief Executive Press: Dorothy Foltz-Gray, Editor;
Stephen Henson, Associate Editor;
Ken Smith, Design Director; Evelyn Ellis, Art Director

Library of Congress Catalog Card Number: 93-061734
Holland, Max
The CEO Goes to Washington
ISBN 1-879736-20-9
ISSN 1060-8923

the chief executive press

The Chief Executive Press presents original short books by distinguished authors on subjects of special importance to the topmost executives of the world's major businesses.

The series is edited and published by Whittle Books, a business unit of Whittle Communications L.P. Books appear several times a year, and the series reflects a broad spectrum of responsible opinions. In each book the opinions expressed are those of the author, not the publisher or the advertiser.

I welcome your comments on this ambitious endeavor.

William S. Rukeyser
Editor in Chief

CONTENTS

INTRODUCTION

Twenty years ago the average U.S. corporate chief executive visited Washington with the same enthusiasm he might have had for trips to a plague-ridden city. His vice-president of governmental affairs, if he had one, was usually an old crony passing out press releases and contributions. Washington was the last place a corporate headhunter looked to find CEO material.

In the '90s CEOs stream into Washington representing not just the Fortune 500 but medium-sized companies as well. "Sometimes National Airport is so full of CEO jets," observes Congressman Jim Cooper, a Tennessee Democrat, "that there's airplane gridlock." The Washington corporate office is no longer the business equivalent of Siberia, and there are more of them—1,500, up 50 percent from 1980. Many CEOs consider a corporate presence in D.C. integral to business. "I don't see how you can operate a large company today without having some liaison in Washington," said David M. Roderick of USX Corporation, the Pittsburgh-based steel and petroleum company.

A tour in government can even serve as a rung on the ladder to the executive suite, especially in the most regulated industries. In 1991 Samuel K. Skinner, George Bush's secretary of Transportation and then chief of staff, became president of Commonwealth Edison. Donald H. Rumsfeld, a former Illinois congressman and Gerald Ford's secretary of Defense, is CEO of Searle pharmaceuticals. Paul H. O'Neill, formerly deputy director of the Office of Management and Budget, is CEO of Alcoa.

The changing relationship between CEOs and Washington is one of the most distinctive alterations in the business-government fabric over the past 20 years. As Edmund T. Pratt Jr., retired CEO of Pfizer pharmaceuticals, observed in *The Lobbyists*, a 1992 book by Jeffrey H. Birnbaum: "What government does is at least as important these days as what your competitor does. Politicians obviously have concluded that business was too important to leave to the businessmen. We've come to the offsetting conclusion: politics is too important just to be left to the politicians."

Regulation is Washington's most obvious intrusion on business, affecting everything from how an enterprise is governed to the market in which it competes. The CEO whose corporation isn't affected by Securities and Exchange Commission guidelines on executive compensation, Department of Defense contracting, Food and Drug Administration regulation of new products, or Environmental Protection Agency rules on pollution must still contend with the Treasury's interpretation of the corporate tax code and the Federal Reserve's macroeconomic policy.

The increasingly competitive global economy is also prompting more CEOs to lobby Washington, particularly when their corporations' access to markets depends on government trade policy. A good example of CEO trade clout occurred in the spring of 1993, when CEOs whose companies do business in Asia formed the vanguard of a new China lobby. Chief executives Frank A. Shrontz of Boeing and George M. C. Fisher, then of Motorola, approached President Clinton while heads of other Fortune 500 companies appealed to Cabinet secretaries. Ultimately they succeeded in extending Beijing's preferential trading status, making possible a stronger American business presence in China.

Even Silicon Valley, that redoubt of entrepreneurship, has realized that its interests are inextricably tied to Washington. As *The New York Times* put it in June 1993, "A visit to Washington to lobby or give testimony is becoming one of the more memorable sidelights of being a high-tech CEO. Twenty years ago, even talking about politics was anathema to the wildcatters of Silicon Valley. What counted was building your chips and beating your neighbor to market."

Yet CEO involvement in Washington politics is not simply a reaction to industry regulation or trade policies. Two other factors stoke high-level attention. One is the history of antagonism between the government and big business; the other is the Washington decision-making process.

The adversarial relationship between government and business in the United States is unique among the industrial nations. Only in America do you find extensive antitrust and regulatory policies and bureaucracies, evidence of a presumption that commerce must be tamed by government. And only in America would a company head provoke a firestorm by claiming, as General Motors president Charles E. "Engine Charlie" Wilson did at a 1953 Senate Armed Services Committee hearing, that "for years I thought what was good for our country was good for General Motors, and vice versa." As Crawford H. Greenewalt, former CEO of Du Pont, once remarked, "Why is it that my American colleagues and I are constantly being taken to court—made to stand trial—for activities that [bring] our counterparts in Britain and other parts of Europe knighthood, peerages, or comparable honors?"

Americans both loathe and worship the corporate engines that bring them prosperity, concludes business historian Alfred D. Chandler. At the turn of the century, the large American market gave rise to businesses unparalleled in size. This new form of enterprise, the corporation, threatened smaller manufacturers, merchants, and entrepreneurs. Soon regulation became the paramount issue in domestic politics, and both parties promised to restrain corporate behemoths. Regulation became the standard response to complex economic problems.

If the antagonism between business and government demands CEO involvement, the porousness of Washington decision-making invites it. Opportunities for intervention abound, and up to a point the CEO can pick the venue: regulatory agencies, Congress, or even the White House. Unlike the business world, where heads roll if CEO decisions are not carried out, in Washington nothing seems final. As three-time Cabinet member George P. Shultz, one of the most experienced officials in Washington, once averred, "Nothing ever gets settled in this town. You have to keep fighting every inch of the way." Business interests can work to pass legislation only to have a House-Senate conference committee render months of careful testimony and lobbying meaningless in minutes. Or painstaking victories on Capitol Hill can be vetoed with the stroke of a president's pen. Just as easily the White House can create a court of last resort, as George Bush did with his Council on Competitiveness, a group that served as a back door for CEOs seeking regulatory redress. It's no surprise that any effort to change policy can prove exasperating.

By most accounts the new era of CEO activity began in the fall of 1972 with the formation of the Business Roundtable, an invitation-only organization of Fortune 500 CEOs and a lobbying force on economic and social issues. Yet nothing dramatized the pivotal role a CEO could play more than the 1980 match between Lee Iacocca, chairman and CEO of Chrysler, and the Carter administration. Iacocca wanted a $1.2 billion loan guarantee that would enable the troubled automaker to construct a new line of compact cars. Critics of federal intervention argued that the government had no business bailing out a corporation suffering from self-inflicted wounds. But Iacocca's blunt talk and Dale Carnegie training mesmerized Washington, and Chrysler got its federal guarantee.

Some manner of bailout was likely unless Iacocca shot himself in the foot. After all, 1980 was an election year, and thousands of workers stood to suffer if Chrysler went belly up. Nevertheless, in the process of championing Chrysler, Iacocca achieved a level of celebrity rare for a CEO. His peers in sectors of manufacturing long identified with America's economic primacy noticed the extraordinary response to Iacocca. As problems in the making for years, such as poor management, outmoded plants and equipment, poor labor relations, and an overvalued dollar, caught up with steel, semiconductor, machine tool, and automobile makers in the early '80s, these manufacturers sought refuge from global competition. They found a receptive audience in Ronald Reagan, who, in contradiction of his laissez-faire vows, proved to be the most protectionist Republican president since Herbert Hoover.

Not every appeal for government largess was as successful as Iacocca's, but during the 1980s activist CEOs had everything to do with the dominant outcomes of laissez-faire for Wall Street on the one hand and protectionism on the other. Accordingly, the media began to pay greater attention to corporate captains. When CEOs fought for a lucrative tax credit in the 1993 tax bill, *The Wall Street Journal* noted, "At times there were more CEOs than lawmakers in the corridors off the floor of the House as the men of steel, oil, and pharmaceuticals came to make their case." For all that, many business leaders who should make their views known stay away. They mistakenly believe that the opportunity to make an impact is small and the chances of getting chewed up, especially by the press, are great.

Despite the seeming ubiquity of CEOs in Washington, relatively few chief executives lobby there. A 1988 survey by the management consulting firm A. T. Kearney showed that only 25 percent of CEOs polled expended at least "moderate efforts" on personal lobbying in Washington. Given the impact of government action on business decisions, the number is surprisingly low, especially since active CEOs said their efforts made a difference. The survey suggests that public policy suffers because many CEOs remain on the sidelines. Observed Democratic Senator David H. Pryor of Arkansas, a 20-year veteran of Washington, "If CEOs do not tell their side of the story, we look at [their silence] as acquiescence or consent for what we are doing."

Even for those CEOs who brave Washington, false assumptions or inexperience with the political process may thwart their quest. What are the best ways to negotiate the system in Washington? Do CEOs have to make large political contributions to open doors? Or hire big-name lawyers and lobbyists to get things done? Do CEOs of medium-sized companies get a hearing or only those of the Fortune 500? Whom do the savviest CEOs see or call, and what are their priorities? Can a CEO be too visible, overidentified with an issue or idea? Are technique, style, and playing the game what matter most? In short, what makes for effectiveness in the halls of power?

This book will attempt to answer these and related questions through the experiences of four CEOs, each of whom has engaged in struggles with the political process and learned how to negotiate Washington. They come from the disparate realms of manufacturing, telecommunications, finance, and energy—industries that waged some of the most intense battles in Washington during the 1980s and that are sure to go on battling through the '90s and beyond.

The profiles depict the range and variety of CEO undertakings in the capital. The first spotlights John A. Young, 61, who retired in November 1992 after 14 years as CEO of Hewlett-Packard Company, the computer and electronic equipment maker based in Palo Alto, California. Young undertook the hardest and most difficult-to-measure task: influencing the marketplace of ideas in Washington. The second profile tells the story of Rene Anselmo, 68, majority owner and CEO of Pan American Satellite (PanAmSat), a Greenwich, Connecticut, satellite communications firm. Anselmo went to Washington to press for relief from regulations that were limiting the marketplace for his company and others like it. The third portrait focuses on Henry R. Kravis, 50, the leading partner in Kohlberg Kravis Roberts & Company, the Wall Street investment banking firm. Kravis worked to accomplish the relatively easy task of getting the government *not* to do something. Procuring inaction can be as valuable as any import quota, million-dollar bailout, or specially crafted tax break. The book concludes with the story of William T. McCormick Jr., 49, CEO of CMS Energy Corporation, based in Dearborn, Michigan. McCormick's struggle was to overhaul existing legislation in a way he maintained would benefit his company, the industry, and the country.

The tactics of the four CEOs differed because each of their agendas had its peculiarities, its own list of dos and don'ts. Still, the profiles reveal common practices that constitute valuable lessons for business leaders trying to influence or understand how Washington works. Some lessons may be surprising: that most CEOs enjoy access to politicians regardless of the size of their companies or campaign contributions, or that the best advice is not necessarily the most expensive. Other lessons may be as mundane as learning that in Washington, as in Peoria, nothing of consequence is accomplished without hard work and perseverance. There is no secret formula for effectiveness. Success involves political skills such as consensus building, compromise, and tenacity. But the loudest and clearest lesson is that CEOs can affect policy in Washington and be comfortable doing it.

When considering the acquisition of a new business jet, you should apply the same financial criteria used to evaluate any major capital investment.

However, it is also important to carefully consider which aircraft other successful companies are buying. Market leadership is a key factor in every industry, but it is especially significant in aviation because product quality, performance, reliability and customer support are such critical factors in the successful operation of a business aircraft.

We are awfully proud of our worldwide leadership at Cessna, because we believe it says more about our line of Citation business jets than any other standard of measurement.

For example, in 1993 we sold more than six out of every 10 business jets delivered worldwide in the light and mid-size categories. This 60 percent market share was an all-time industry record.

In December alone, we delivered more business jets than all but one competitor delivered during the entire year. That degree of market dominance, in our view, is the best possible evidence of customer satisfaction.

With more than 2,100 Citations already operating in 63 countries, a rapidly expanding line of Citations and a company-wide commitment to support our customers, we are confident that our worldwide leadership will continue well into the 21st century.

Sincerely yours,

Russell W. Meyer, Jr.

Russell W. Meyer, Jr.
Chairman and Chief Executive Officer
Cessna Aircraft Company

Cessna Aircraft Company · One Cessna Boulevard · Wichita, Kansas 67215 · 316/941-7400

Cessna
A Textron Company

Chapter One

ON THE
COMPETITIVENESS EDGE

If federal officials were to name the most effective CEOs of the past decade, John A. Young would undoubtedly top the list. During his tenure at the helm of Hewlett-Packard, Young was not content with merely advancing his company's interests. Beginning in 1983, he prodded Washington to address what he considered the greatest threat to American prosperity since the Depression: declining economic competitiveness.

Ten years later competitiveness has become not just a buzzword but a pivotal political issue. The 1992 presidential election was largely a referendum on America's economic future, and Young was a catalyst in establishing the coalition between Democrats and high-technology industry that helped Bill Clinton win the presidency. If business and government go on to forge a new relationship, Young can share authorship. While bringing about this sea change in the business-government relationship, Young increased Hewlett-Packard's considerable access to and credibility with Washington decision-makers and oversaw a company boom. During Young's 14-year reign, which ended with his retirement in 1992, Hewlett-Packard's sales increased from $1.8 billion to $16.4 billion.

Young first focused on the competitiveness issue after a game of tennis in the spring of 1983. He was attending a meeting of the Business Council, an organization for members of corporate senior management, at Hot Springs, Virginia. Featured speaker Edwin L. Harper, President Reagan's

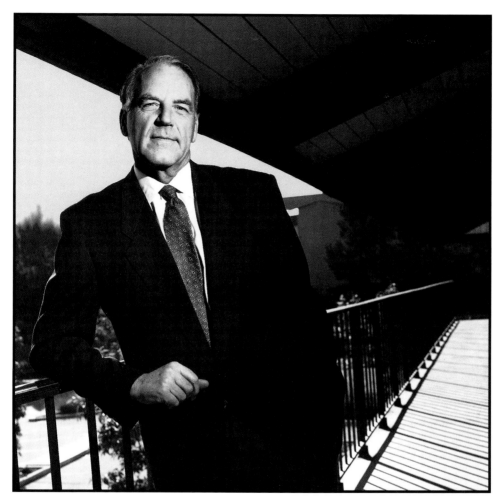

JOHN A. YOUNG
former CEO, Hewlett-Packard

domestic policy adviser, discussed the government's role in research and development. As CEO of the original high-tech Silicon Valley start-up, Young listened closely. Hewlett-Packard was holding its own in the marketplace, but Young was disturbed that the U.S. share of the consumer electronics market had fallen from nearly 100 percent in 1970 to less than 5 percent by the mid-'80s. He ruminated about the environment in which manufacturers compete and wondered why U.S. makers of integrated circuits used by companies such as HP were losing market share as well. "I got interested in this subject simply as a CEO," said Young, "thinking, *Why are we losing to the Japanese?*" It didn't take a wizard to recognize that if the trend was not reversed, Hewlett-Packard might suffer. "I was looking forward to hearing about [the government's policy]," he recalled, "because it surprised me that there was such a thing."

After the speech Young joined Harper for a tennis match. The game was less memorable than their verbal volleying. "I was kind of kidding Harper after his talk. 'Gee, you don't have a strategy [for commercial R&D] after all,'" says Young. "We got to bantering about what [such a strategy] would take, what some of the ideas should be, and what the issues were."

At the time, the Reagan White House had a problem. It was facing the 1984 election and the economy was emerging from the most severe recession in 50 years. Many companies, particularly manufacturers, had suffered serious losses of market share to overseas competitors, and the Democrats intended to make the hemorrhaging of American manufacturing an election issue.

Reagan could attack the Democrats' calls for industrial policy as central planning in disguise, but he still needed something to assuage voters. So he did what most presidents do when presented with a difficult situation. He set up an advisory panel to study the problem.

Edwin Harper, in charge of setting up the President's Commission on Industrial Competitiveness, asked Young to lead the panel, hardly a surprise given Hewlett-Packard's reputation as a company "whose blend of advanced technology and enlightened management defined Silicon Valley," as *Business Week* put it. In 1938 William R. Hewlett and David Packard raised $538 to build audio oscillators in a garage for their first customer, Walt Disney; by the time Harper and Young met in 1983, HP employed 68,000, had become the largest maker of electronic test and measurement instruments, and was on its way to becoming a major computer manufacturer. Young understood and embraced the political nature of the commission, convinced that the early version of industrial policy advocated by the Democrats gave the government too much economic control.

Chairing the commission was Young's Washington debut, extending the Hewlett-Packard tradition of involvement. David Packard had served as deputy secretary of Defense in the Nixon administration from 1969 to 1971 and in 1985 and '86 headed the Packard Commission, which studied defense procurement. Packard encouraged Young to head the Commission on Competitiveness, and in June 1983 the White House announced his appointment.

If the Reagan administration thought it had found a pliable and predictable chairman, it was mistaken. Young had no intention of delivering a precooked conclusion. An electrical engineer by training, he intended to approach the assignment with the same quiet, steady attitude that had taken him to the top of Hewlett-Packard in 25 years. He was known within

HP for preparation, patience, and integrity, and these characteristics soon permeated the commission as well.

Young sought the counsel of David P. Gardner, then president of the University of California system. Gardner had just finished heading the National Commission on Excellence in Education, which produced "A Nation At Risk," the landmark study that galvanized public attention on the decline of American schools. Gardner had a lot to tell Young about commission dynamics: what to expect, what to avoid, how to get the right mix of views and personalities, and how to handle dissenting views.

Young also set out to find an aide who knew Washington. He recruited Tom Uhlman, a Stanford Business School graduate who had served as a midlevel official in the Department of Education. Uhlman's experience paid immediate dividends. After taking soundings in Washington, recalled Uhlman, "I came back pretty strong to Young that we needed to have independence or else we were going to be set up going into an election year." Uhlman also perceived that the proposed membership was not broad enough, with too few representatives from the technology community and none from organized labor. Young talked with Edwin Meese, counselor to the president and later attorney general, who offered to find the labor representatives himself. After two weeks, according to Young, Meese called back and said the White House didn't know any labor leaders.

Young resumed the labor search himself and also persuaded the CEOs of several high-tech companies and the former head of Morgan Stanley & Company, the investment banking firm, to join the commission. He persuaded the administration to give the commission its own staff and budget. Uhlman then recruited independent-minded civil servants from various agencies for all but the top staff position. By the time it sat down to work, the commission had achieved a measure of independence.

With the membership in place, Young reviewed the literature on competitiveness, insisting on a firsthand education. He examined one report published in 1983 by the Business-Higher Education Forum, a group of 40 Fortune 100 CEOs and 40 university presidents. The catalyst for the report had been Japan's increasing economic power. The study coined an umbrella phrase, *economic competitiveness*, for the issues it addressed—from education and worker training to trade and technology policy.

Young found the forum's findings balanced, thoughtful, and comprehensive, and the commission decided to use the report as a base line. Of course, before defining the problem, Young had to forge a consensus among his commission members, each of whom had a different understanding of competitiveness, although they did agree on one point. "Practically everybody, in starting out, said, 'Gee, if only our exports were higher, that's it,'" recalled Young. It took six months to agree that competitiveness referred much more broadly to the ability of American companies and workers to excel in the global marketplace.

By early 1984 Young and his colleagues decided not to meet the pre-November deadline agreed upon with the administration. Commission members feared the White House might stifle any less-than-optimistic findings before an election. Young's request for a delay suited the administration because political pressure had dissipated. The economy was recovering, and the Democratic candidates trailed Reagan in the polls. Commission members turned to a new goal: producing a report that could influence Reagan's second-term agenda.

Young secured the best possible forum for presenting the finished report, a Cabinet meeting in early February 1985. Young conducted the briefing himself, using an overhead projector to illustrate the commission's conclusions. "Global Competition: The New Reality" was not calculated to please. There were profound systemic problems in the American economy, the report claimed. The United States was "losing its ability to compete in the world's markets."

Young gored some sacred cows, most notably military spending. For 40 years the government had put military technology first and expected commercial benefits to trickle down. Young said that military R&D was draining America's stock of scientific and technological talent. And in 1983, although the government supported 884 industrial advisory commissions engaging 17,980 people from business, trade associations, labor, academia, and the government, these sources of advice and expertise met infrequently and had little impact. What the federal government needed, Young told President Reagan and his assembled Cabinet officers, was a competitiveness strategy.

The commission's recommendations were met with apathy and skepticism. After all, "Global Competition" was a politically and ideologically brazen report, especially given Reagan's landslide win in November. Reagan scribbled his reaction in a note to Secretary of State George Shultz. If the United States has such economic problems, Reagan asked, why did all those foreign countries still want to be like America?

Responses from others in the administration were no more reassuring. Donald T. Regan, the newly appointed chief of staff, scarcely bothered to hide his hostility to a report that recommended more federal spending. Regan argued that second-term priorities had been set and there was no money for the programs endorsed by the commission. The Commerce Department, not the White House, released the report, a send-off that summed up the administration's tepid response.

The business community reacted more positively. Yet Young found that CEOs in manufacturing still believed competitiveness was largely a question of U.S. export performance, and lagging exports, in turn, were a function of the overvalued dollar. When Reagan devalued the dollar in 1985, the CEOs felt certain the competitiveness issue was settled.

But Young believed that currency fixes were no panacea for embedded problems such as record trade deficits, flagging American inventiveness, an inability to make commercial use of military technology, and inadequate investment in education and infrastructure. Although forewarned that commission reports "go directly to the Smithsonian without going through any heads or hands," as one former commission head put it, Young wasn't prepared to see his report dismissed. He was convinced that competitiveness affected not only Hewlett-Packard's long-term fortunes, but the nation's future.

A few months after the release of "Global Competition," Alexander B. Trowbridge Jr., president of the National Association of Manufacturers and a Commerce secretary during the Johnson administration, stopped to see Young at Hewlett-Packard headquarters in Palo Alto. The competitiveness problem was getting worse, he told Young, and something had to be done. You are the leader, said Trowbridge. When everybody talks about competitiveness, they talk about you. How about doing more through a new organization? Young polled his fellow commission members, and many agreed to keep the competitiveness issue alive until 1989, when a more receptive administration might take office. Like the commission, this organization would reflect the national interest, not the narrow agenda of high-tech manufacturers.

Young sent Tom Uhlman on another scouting mission to Washington to see about establishing a small organization with a modest budget and part-time director. Uhlman told Young that if he wanted results, the new organization had to have an ample budget and a full-time director and staff. Young borrowed a nonprofit shell that the National Association of Manufacturers had already established with the Internal Revenue Service, and Trowbridge kicked in $75,000. Young began recruiting the heads of corporations, universities, and labor unions to join on a sliding-dues scale; Fortune 500 companies paid the top annual rate of $15,000. Within weeks he had won the allegiance of prominent business, academic, and labor leaders such as Donald E. Petersen, then CEO of Ford, Paul E. Gray, then president of MIT, and Morton Bahr, president of the Communications Workers of America. Young asked the members to make a three-year commitment, emphasizing his intention to "sunset" the council by 1989 if it didn't work. "I told everybody, 'I don't know if this is a good idea,'" Young recalled. "'But I need this window of commitment. After three years, if the council's going nowhere, we probably ought to get rid of it. If it's making progress, maybe it should be continued.'"

The Council on Competitiveness opened for business in August 1986. Its charter dedicated the council to "improving the ability of U.S.

RESEARCH INDICATES THAT OFTEN,
THE ROAD TO SUCCESS ISN'T PAVED AT ALL.

A recent study by Arthur Andersen, a leading global accounting firm, showed that on average, the performance of companies purchasing and operating aircraft is far superior to those who do not. Of *Fortune* magazine's 50 companies with the highest total return to investors, 92% operate aircraft. Of *Business Week's* "Productivity Pacesetters," 80% own or operate business aircraft.

"No plane, no gain," is more than an advertising slogan for the business aviation industry. It is usually the simple truth.

THE SENSIBLE CITATIONS

Cessna
A Textron Company

industry and its workers to compete in world markets while raising living standards at home." Young selected Alan H. Magazine to be the council's first president. As director of the Business-Higher Education Forum, Magazine had helped coin the phrase *economic competitiveness*. His first day at the office was eerily quiet, his desk bare except for a telephone, legal pad, and pen. Within a few days, however, an article in *The Washington Post* announced the council's formation, and Magazine was swamped with calls from journalists, Capitol Hill aides, think-tank researchers, and business, academic, and labor leaders eager to join. Even in a town glutted with advocacy groups, the council was evoking excitement. Besides the participation of world-class competitors like Hewlett-Packard, Motorola, and Xerox, Magazine said, "the reason this thing flew was John Young." "Global Competition" had established Young as the top business leader on the competitiveness issue.

In April 1987 the council released "America's Competitive Crisis: Confronting the New Reality," a paper intended to introduce the organization and gauge the public's response. To change the national agenda the council had to make news. "If you can't stay in the news with your ideas," observed Magazine, "you might as well not exist."

The council soon recognized a barometer: the increasing use of *competitiveness* as a buzzword. In the council's first year, whenever Magazine gave a speech he began by explaining that the council was not associated with the Olympics, and no, he was not there to talk about how to win more gold medals. After one year, however, Magazine no longer had to do that. "I'd test the audience and say, 'Tell me what [competitiveness] issues we should be concerned about.' The audience would throw out productivity, quality of products, and they'd keep going and going. They knew because of all the national publicity."

There were other signs that the council's cause was entering the mainstream. President Reagan had studiously avoided speaking the word *competitiveness*; to do so implied that the U.S. economy was not competitive. Nevertheless, he used the *C* word during his 1987 State of the Union address. The council took this utterance as a vindication of its effort, although no one believed the mention was anything more than rhetoric, given the administration's lack of interest.

As the council's message gained visibility, recalled Magazine, "John Young became more comfortable with his role as chairman, more comfortable bringing these people together, and more comfortable speaking out." Unlike many advocacy groups, the council was not driven by the agenda of the staff. If anything, the executive committee, led by Young, spun the staff. Young pored through the information provided by the staff, analyzing it and coming back with questions. He became famous for an "iron" backside during board meetings when members hammered out council positions. Young "didn't ram things down people's throats," said Magazine. "He let the force of the arguments, the force of the information, drive the process and the results."

Young's stature and visibility also paid dividends for Hewlett-Packard. As with most multinational corporations, HP's legislative agenda was dominated by tax and trade issues. The company's lobbyists made the most of Young's reputation as a "white hat," using his access to important officials to press their agenda. Young acknowledges that as the lead spokesman for competitiveness, he greatly improved "HP's access and credibility and ability to make points with key legislators."

Young's experience in mobilizing a coalition around competitiveness convinced him of the value of Washington alliances. During the 1980s, Young and his Hewlett-Packard colleagues helped found two coalitions that furthered the agendas of Hewlett-Packard and similar companies. One was the Council on Research and Technology (CORETECH), which grew to represent more than 150 research-intensive companies, universities, and other institutions on tax issues related to investment and research and development. CORETECH successfully fought a Treasury regulation that would have raised taxes on the domestic R&D efforts of HP and other U.S. companies with overseas facilities. Young was also the founder and leading force in the Computer Systems Policy Project, a mini-Business Roundtable made up of CEOs from 13 large computer companies, whose aims included removing barriers to high-tech exports in the aftermath of the Cold War.

During the 1988 presidential campaign, the Council on Competitiveness embarked on its most ambitious effort to date: to make competitiveness an election issue. It scoured every camp to find advisers willing to adopt the council's agenda. It also publicized the major candidates' views on competitiveness. In addition, just after the start of the fall campaign, the council released its second major report in an attempt to influence election-year discourse. "This report should destroy some comforting illusions about America's technological leadership," said Young at the press conference for "Picking Up the Pace."

This latest effort marked a shift in emphasis by Young and the council. Previous reports, going back to the commission's original tome, focused on persuading readers that there was a competitiveness problem. "Picking Up the Pace" did too, but it also revealed detailed proposals that became the council's litany for the next four years. The council called upon the federal government to lower the cost of capital by controlling the deficit while redoubling efforts to open foreign markets to high-tech American exports. The report also called for more federal investment in the nation's universities and laboratories and a larger, more coordinated role for the government in promoting manufacturing and technological advances. This second proposal subsumed many suggestions, from streamlining federal regulations to loosening antitrust laws so that U.S. companies could work together to develop basic technologies.

In a speech a few weeks after the report's release, George Bush alluded to the need for a technology policy and endorsed several of the report's recommendations. "We had no idea that Bush was going to do it, although I don't think for a minute that he opened the covers of our report," recalled Alan Magazine. For days the council was flooded with requests for what now appeared to be a partial blueprint for the incoming Bush administration. Of course, everyone at the council recognized the difference between campaign rhetoric and actual governing. If Bush was a believer in the council's agenda, it would become evident only after he moved into the Oval Office.

Initially the new administration made several encouraging decisions. Bush added the evaluation of technology to the duties of his science and technology adviser, D. Allan Bromley, and elevated the position to Cabinet rank. He also formed a White House Council on Competitiveness to spur business growth. And access to top officials improved. A council delegation met with Vice-President Dan Quayle for 30 minutes in February and later with top commerce and trade officials. Commerce Secretary Robert A. Mosbacher, in particular, became a strong ally in the council's push for a comprehensive federal strategy.

Within a year, however, high hopes became dashed expectations. An elegant White House lunch for the council's executive committee, hosted by Quayle in the Indian Treaty Room, summed up the attitude of the Bush administration. Recalled Magazine, "We brought in a Who's Who of top corporate and academic leaders in America, who were there to talk about major issues and problems of competitiveness and kept regaling Quayle about recommendations we had. Every now and then he would look up from his food, and he'd ask a question, just to get it going. He didn't make one declarative sentence the entire time we were there. It was as though he didn't understand these issues and couldn't care less."

The administration mimicked Quayle's indifference. The Council on Competitiveness turned into an appeals court for businesses burdened by federal regulations, especially environmental edicts. Restrictions such as product liability laws were the source of America's competitiveness problems, or so the White House believed. And Robert Mosbacher proved no match for John H. Sununu, Bush's chief of staff and a foe of industrial policy. After Mosbacher urged federal support for high-definition television systems, reported *Business Week*, Sununu summoned Mosbacher to his office and rebuked him for "sounding like Michael Dukakis." Craig Fields, an outspoken Pentagon official respected by the council, lost his job after advocating federal support for technologies, as did Deputy Commerce Secretary Thomas Murrin. The council's monthly newsletter quoted Allan Bromley, who said, in essence, that money for government intervention by "brute force" was not available, was not likely to be available, and if it were available "it was unlikely that such an approach would work." The assertive leadership Young had yearned for in a president was not forthcoming.

As hope for substantial change faded, Young sought incremental gains. By late 1989 he had developed a better understanding of how Washington worked and resigned himself to some capital realities. Unlike change in the business world, progress in Washington is glacial. Without presidential leadership, creating even small changes in the bureaucracy takes consistent pressure. "We're probably lucky that public policies don't jump around," said Young. "We need the kind of stability you can depend upon." Influencing public policy, he discovered, took patience, determination, timing, and credibility. To accomplish his goals, he had to be prepared for every opportunity.

Young found four top officials to work with: Richard G. Darman, director of the Office of Management and Budget; Michael J. Boskin, head of the Council of Economic Advisers; Roger B. Porter, the chief domestic policy adviser in the White House; and most important, Allan Bromley. Through frequent meetings with these officials, Young established relationships that led to slow but measurable changes in John Sununu's hands-off approach. Bromley initiated an interagency review of government policy on applied technologies—such as robotics and computer-aided design and manufacturing—hoping to draw federal dollars to technology development and not just pure science. Bromley also wanted to discover which generic technologies were critical for economic growth and military strength. Meanwhile Darman, the czar of federal spending, instigated a government-wide survey of research-and-development expenditures, searching for ways to get more commercial mileage out of every federal buck. Young embraced these efforts, although he felt the cooperation came grudgingly. Bromley's progress was slow, and the council felt sure that Sununu bullied him on key issues. As Jeff Bingaman, a Democratic senator from New Mexico, put it, "There is still a raging dispute...in the White House over the government's role" in industry.

The council, convinced its efforts were beginning to produce results, unanimously extended its mandate until 1992. Its budget approached $1 million and 150 chief executives had joined. Its success, coupled with John Young's need to attend to Hewlett-Packard, prompted a change in leadership. "For some time, I have been sensitive to the possibility of the council becoming too closely identified with any single person," Young said. "The focus should always remain on the council." So in December 1990 he turned over the reins to George Fisher, then CEO of Motorola.

Young remained active on the executive committee and was instrumental in shaping and promoting the council's third and most significant report.

"Gaining New Ground," released in March 1991, became the most requested of the council's five major reports, with more than 7,500 copies distributed. The report listed the technologies most likely to yield new manufacturing processes and products over the next decade, distilling more than six years of Young's thinking about technology and the federal government. Federal agencies had compiled lists of key technologies before. What made "Gaining New Ground" unique was that its source was business. Young recalled the novelty of the exercise, particularly in relation to computers, one of the sectors he knows best: "It was the first time ever that the chief technologists of 12 computer companies had gotten together to talk about where we stood as an industry."

"Gaining New Ground" also took inventory of America's standing in world markets and presented the first private-sector consensus on resurrecting U.S. economic leadership. The report called for a marked departure from an industrial policy shaped by the Cold War. "Today's leading-edge technologies in microelectronics, computers, and telecommunications are found not in Defense Department laboratories but in private industry," the report stressed. As Young liked to remind people, "You probably saw the Patriot missile during Desert Storm. It's got a microprocessor that's from the Dark Ages."

Weeks after the council published "Gaining New Ground," the White House released its own technology policy statement. Young was pleased that Bush's list of critical technologies was identical to the council's. But the policy statement had come only after arduous and time-consuming debate, and it was a limited document with no guarantee that anything resembling the council's recommendations would be put into practice. Young's sometime allies in the White House, Darman and Boskin, added a sentence distancing the White House from its own report. Such sensitivity was not surprising given the Bush administration's dislike of federal industrial policies. Yet the setback grated on Young, who believed that the challenge was not in generating a list of technologies but in enacting a long-term policy to foster them.

Although both Democrats and Republicans were to blame for what Young called the "decision-making gridlock in Washington," Young put the onus on the president. Bush was unwilling to use the bully pulpit of the presidency to push for changes in economic policy, and friction inside his administration dissipated whatever energy existed. After Robert Mosbacher succeeded in establishing an advanced technology program inside the Commerce Department, industrial-policy opponents ensured that the program's budget was minuscule, and lower-level officials risked losing their jobs if they pushed industrial policy too hard—as Fields and Murrin had before them.

The situation improved after Sununu resigned in December 1991, but much of Bush's technology program still consisted of whatever congressional Democrats enacted over the administration's resistance. Critical components of Young's agenda, such as a government policy encouraging the application of new technology to industry, were missing. Other goals, such as Bush's vow to be the "education president," never produced results. Young believed that "the real force in driving things ahead never quite seemed to be there."

The 1992 election marked the third presidential campaign since Young began his focus on competitiveness. Although still a Republican, he no longer thought of competitiveness as a partisan issue. Young was eager to help any candidate who might support his agenda.

Among the first to contact Young was Bill Clinton, the governor of Arkansas. When Young met with Clinton in the summer of 1991, he was struck by the governor's command of the issues and the similarity of their views. Clinton's record of support for a limited national industrial policy dated back more than 10 years. He believed technology was the key in a world dominated by an economic rather than a Cold War. Finally, Young was impressed by Clinton's intellectual capacity and commitment to change. Young had never seen a president or vice-president so quick to grasp ideas and technical details. Clinton absorbed everything that Young and his council sent him and appeared open to making the council's agenda part of his campaign agenda.

Still, Young looked carefully before declaring his support for the Democrat. During an August meeting in New York, two dozen CEOs questioned Clinton about his plan to cut the deficit while increasing infrastructure investment. Young voiced doubts about the calculations that went into Clinton's economic plan, "Putting People First." The CEO had reviewed the numbers during his flight from California, and they didn't add up. Clinton instructed Ira C. Magaziner, one of his top economic aides and later his medical policy adviser, to allay Young's concerns.

When Clinton asked for his endorsement, Young answered that he would first have to see the candidate's policy paper on technology. Since Clinton had none, the campaign drafted Young, along with Lawrence Ellison of Oracle Systems and John Sculley of Apple, to help write one. "Technology: The Engine of Economic Growth" was barely distinguishable from the council's "Gaining New Ground." The paper "made a hell of a lot of sense," said Young. The Clinton campaign was making high-tech investment a theme, while the Bush campaign, which had been given a similar chance to adopt council proposals, was far less receptive.

Young's interest in Clinton was duplicated by many CEOs of high-technology companies who believed the economy was experiencing a sea change that called for more vigorous leadership. With the fall 1992 release of "Engine of Growth," Young, Ellison, Sculley, and 28 other CEOs of high-tech companies endorsed the Democratic ticket. "To be successful as a nation," said Young at a press conference in San Jose, "we have to forge a private sector-public sector partnership." Silicon Valley had traditionally been a GOP fortress, fiercely attached to the ideas of entrepreneurship, free markets, and minimal government involvement. The CEO endorsements of Clinton indicated grave weakness in Bush's political base: the price he paid for his scant attention to technology policy.

Young's endorsement came as no surprise to his colleagues, who knew his commitment to the competitiveness issue. But not all of Young's peers approved. "The surprise is that some thoughtful corporate leaders like John Young have decided to bet on a Clinton presidency," said Jerry J. Jasinowski, Alexander Trowbridge's successor as president of the National Association of Manufacturers. The sharpest criticism came from David Packard, who suggested in a letter to the *San Jose Mercury News* that Young's endorsement was linked to political ambition. If Clinton won, Packard explained, Young would have a chance of becoming secretary of the Commerce Department, the traditional voice of business in Washington. Young and "many other good friends in the Silicon Valley industry have been caught in the updraft of Bill Clinton's hot-air balloon," wrote Packard.

For a few weeks after Clinton's victory it seemed that Packard had been right about Young's aims. But Young's commitment to competitiveness was not to be confused with Potomac Fever, and he took himself out of the running. "I have determined that an official role might create the appearance of a conflict of interest because of my financial holdings," Young told the press, adding that he would find other ways to pursue what had become his passionate hobby.

With a sympathetic administration in place, Young began to concentrate on two aims. One is to prevent carefully nurtured ideas from becoming just another form of pork barrel politics, and the other is to warn against wild-eyed plans that might excessively inject the government into the free market. The latter concern, Young believes, will develop only if business people refuse to participate in the political process. "Fortunately, what I detect among my colleagues is a great willingness to get involved," noted Young. He has indicated to Clinton that he would serve on a successor commission to Reagan's Commission on Industrial Competitiveness and help realize goals such as a 21st-century information infrastructure involving fiber optics and high-speed computer networks. And he will not let the Council on Competitiveness dissolve. "I think the council has a role to play as long as that agenda is alive and needs strategic help," said Young. "The Congress and White House are tactical, they are event-driven, and they need people who have time to develop ideas and test them, to be a resource." Young and other council members have talked of establishing an offshoot of the council that could lobby, not just advocate, certain positions.

Regardless of what Young goes on to achieve, the changes he has wrought are formidable. Fifteen members of the Council on Competitiveness, including Young, participated in Clinton's Little Rock economic summit six weeks after the election. When, a month later, Clinton unveiled his economic program before Congress, with its emphasis on deficit reduction, investment in infrastructure, and competitiveness, it read like a page out of the council hymnal. David Barram, the Apple vice-president who helped engineer Silicon Valley's endorsement of Clinton, became the deputy secretary of the Commerce Department, and Kent H. Hughes, president of the council, became an associate deputy secretary. Clinton's $17 billion technology initiative, unveiled in February 1993, signaled an end to the laissez-faire ideology that catapulted Young into action in '83. The Clinton administration "is taking competitiveness more seriously than [did] President Bush," Young observed.

In the view of political analyst Kevin Phillips, if Young's analysis, developed over 10 years, is the correct prescription for what ails the American economy and if President Clinton follows it faithfully, a new consensus favoring industrial policy could redefine business-government relations for a generation.

John Young's story is striking testimony to what a CEO can achieve in Washington—particularly when he approaches the capital with more than an engineer's mentality. A good engineer studies a problem, then develops a solution and expects to persuade everyone else on the merits alone. When Young finished working for the Commission on Industrial Competitiveness in 1985, he could have folded his tent and left town, content that he had developed the right answer; never mind that he couldn't persuade Washington. Instead he learned how to make things happen in the capital, not in the "just do it" manner of a corporate leader, but through the back and forth of politics. He learned to appreciate incremental success, to establish and advance an agenda—and to be comfortable in that role. Most important, he helped rivet government and national attention on a crucial issue, America's ability to compete in the 21st century.

SCHEDULE A BUSINESS MEETING NEXT DOOR TO THE SOUND BARRIER.

Inside, it is an elegant conference room. Quiet. Abundantly spacious.
Beautifully appointed. With soft leather recliners, individual television
monitors, and a private dressing room.

Outside, it is slicing through the sky at more than 870 feet per second.
Mach .90. One-tenth of a point below the speed of sound.

The remarkable new Citation X. Reservations will be accepted soon
for demonstration flights in 1995. And they'll be going fast.

THE SENSIBLE CITATIONS

Cessna
A Textron Company

Chapter Two

DECONSTRUCTING A MONOPOLY

John Young is a striking example of how one CEO can influence the national agenda. Yet his quest is atypical. Young sought broad changes that aligned with Hewlett-Packard's interests. Most CEOs go to Washington to convince the capital that their company's interest is also in the national interest.

This motive led Rene Anselmo to Washington. As CEO of PanAmSat, a Connecticut-based satellite communications company, Anselmo was vying to unlock the monopoly on satellite communications held by the Communications Satellite Corporation (Comsat) and Intelsat, the international consortium to which Comsat belongs. Although in 1984 President Reagan had officially declared privately run satellite systems to be in the national interest, Anselmo's negotiations in Washington would not be easy. His struggle for regulatory relief would require much of what had been required of Young: time, a skilled team, and acceptance of Washington's tendency to compromise.

The struggle Anselmo faced is similar to an earlier battle between a combative businessman and a communications monopoly. In 1968 William G. McGowan, CEO of Microwave Communications Inc., challenged the AT&T monopoly, and his battle lasted 16 years in the courts, in Congress, and before the Federal Communications Commission. At times McGowan's employees joked that MCI amounted to "a law firm with an antenna on the roof." By 1984, however, antitrust lawsuits brought by MCI and the Justice Department had shattered AT&T's monopoly;

RENE ANSELMO
CEO, Pan American Satellite Corporation

McGowan won a $113 million verdict and the right to compete. At McGowan's death in 1992, MCI was the second-largest U.S. long-distance telephone company, with revenues of $8.4 billion.

McGowan's campaign made Anselmo's possible; it introduced the idea of competition into the telecommunications industry. In several respects, though, Anselmo's uphill climb to make PanAmSat the MCI of the satellite world has been even steeper than McGowan's efforts against AT&T. The Bell monopoly was government-sanctioned, whereas the monopoly Anselmo would battle was government-created. McGowan had only U.S. law to worry about, whereas Anselmo has had to contend with the laws of every country in which he wants to do business, as well as the Intelsat consortium, which enjoys special privileges and immunities and once seemed as immutable as death and taxes. But Anselmo has succeeded despite these odds, and one measure of his effectiveness is that Comsat would not talk about him or PanAmSat on or off the record. As one industry analyst told *Via Satellite*, a trade publication, Comsat and Intelsat have "held the monopoly position, and in terms of the marketplace there's nowhere to go but down."

Anselmo's case illustrates a truism about doing business in the capital. If one thinks of Washington as a pond, then any pebble thrown in by one element—Congress, the media, or the FCC—causes ripples. As Phillip L. Spector, one of Anselmo's lawyers, observed, "There is an absolute relationship between what happens on the Hill, what happens in the press, and what happens in the agencies. One is constantly reminded that Washington is a small town, and you can't get away from the relationships that exist among people who work together on a daily basis."

Rene Anselmo, a native of Medford, Massachusetts, flew 37 missions as a Marine tail gunner in World War II. If his flair for the dramatic isn't instinctive, he developed it while studying theater after the war at the University of Chicago. For the next 11 years, he lived in Mexico City, where he dubbed TV shows such as *I Love Lucy* into Spanish. In 1961 Anselmo returned to the United States and, with other investors, bought a bankrupt UHF station and turned it into the Spanish International Network (SIN). Via this 23-station network he funneled programming from Mexico to America's growing Hispanic population. He ran this country's largest Spanish-language network for 25 years, until the FCC questioned the control exercised by his Mexican partners. Anselmo sold his stake in 1986 for $100 million and, seeing that the price and availability of international satellite communications had not kept pace with the technology, plowed the money into a two-year-old venture called the Pan American Satellite Corporation.

The prehistory of PanAmSat's struggle dates back to 1958, when the Soviet Union launched the first sputnik. Space became another Cold War battleground, and the U.S. government was determined that satellite communications contribute to the free flow of information. In 1962 landmark U.S. legislation created the framework for a global satellite communications system. Comsat was born as the U.S. affiliate of Intelsat, a worldwide consortium of the Western world's telecommunications authorities. For a technology still in infancy, a government-supported monopoly made sense. Competing private systems seemed neither desirable nor feasible. For one thing, rockets and satellites were expensive, and governments had built and owned the only ones in existence. And a monopoly had the advantage of uniform rates and services.

Intelsat was a success, its operations untroubled by politics. Eventually

110 nations belonged to the consortium, which operated 15 satellites and handled about two-thirds of all international telephony and most international television transmissions. By the 1980s, however, almost everything about the technology had changed except the international regime. The use of fiber-optic cables for transatlantic calls, the availability of rockets and satellites to private companies, and the reduced cost yet increased demand for data transmission all altered the original argument for a monopoly. It no longer made sense technically, and some private companies believed they could provide new and improved services, cut costs, and make a healthy profit. In 1984 a handful of companies, PanAmSat among them, petitioned the FCC for the right to establish satellite systems that would compete with Intelsat.

Comsat-Intelsat's lobby argued that PanAmSat and its kind wanted only to skim off the most lucrative sectors of the international market. An equitable, irreplaceable international system would be destroyed, the consortium charged. Ultimately, however, the Reagan White House decided that greater competition would enhance service and that privately owned satellite systems were in the national interest. The days of monopoly seemed numbered.

But it took another three years and millions in legal and lobbying fees before PanAmSat could launch its own satellite. Anselmo claimed that Comsat and Intelsat erected barriers whenever possible by encouraging potential customers to boycott PanAmSat and by delaying the consultations that Intelsat required with all competing companies to avoid disrupting transmissions and to coordinate satellite orbits. Acquiring "landing rights" for the signals beamed from space to various countries was especially troublesome. Recalled Anselmo, "No sooner would we make a step than the Intelsat squads would be all over" trying to undo the deal. And without provable demand, raising the necessary capital was impossible. Far from deterring Anselmo, such obstacles only lit a fire in the volatile, chain-smoking CEO. Borrowing a phrase that Ronald Reagan had applied to the Soviet Union, Anselmo began referring to Intelsat as "the evil communications empire."

In June 1988, while Anselmo was recovering from quintuple bypass surgery, a French rocket put a 2,700 pound RCA-built satellite into orbit for PanAmSat. Anselmo had obtained the satellite at a bargain-basement price after the original buyer canceled the order. He nicknamed the world's first privately owned satellite *Simón Bolívar* after the South American liberator. *Bolívar* cost $85 million to launch, $66 million of which came out of Anselmo's pocket. Insured for only half the cost, Anselmo would have lost tens of millions if the satellite had failed.

The direction of events after *Bolívar* went into orbit suggests that Anselmo's good-versus-evil view of his struggle was not farfetched.

Although Anselmo had not expected to break even for six years, by 1990 PanAmSat was earning $600,000 on revenues of $16.7 million, and its customers included ABC, Chile's Compañia de Telefonos, the European Broadcasting Union, and Argentina's Television Federal.

Anselmo was convinced that PanAmSat could grow even faster by dismantling the barriers to new satellite technologies. Circumstances surrounding the 1989 collapse of the Berlin Wall bolstered this conviction. CBS television wanted to broadcast the event live, but its new uplink equipment had not yet been licensed by the West German telecommunications authority, a member of Intelsat. CBS, which wanted to use the PanAmSat satellite to transmit to the U.S., pleaded with Anselmo to help circumvent the licensing delay. Anselmo tracked down the West German telecommunications minister and got permission for CBS to use the new uplink equipment. As a result Americans witnessed one of the momentous events of postwar history live via PanAmSat. But the problems CBS and PanAmSat had setting up the transmission proved "the whole rottenness of this stupid situation," Anselmo told *Satellite Communications*, a monthly trade magazine. "It's inconceivable, especially to someone from the United States, that any television station would be unable to select and use whatever uplink capability it thought was in its best interests." Anselmo vowed to force Intelsat to operate on the same commercial basis as PanAmSat—without special privileges.

Anselmo's main target became Intelsat's monopoly of telephony. After Reagan's 1984 decision favoring private satellite systems, the FCC had ruled that such systems still could not compete with Intelsat in making international telephone connections; in industry jargon, access to public switched networks (PSN) was denied. Connecting telephone circuits accounted for almost 75 percent of all international satellite revenues, and the FCC deemed this large slice of Intelsat's business sacrosanct. But after competing with Comsat and Intelsat for five years, Anselmo was convinced that these protected revenues enabled Intelsat to engage in predatory pricing. In July 1990 Anselmo's lawyers, Henry Goldberg and Phil Spector, filed a petition with the FCC asking for access to PSN. If approved, the petition would end Intelsat's monopoly.

Against Comsat's team of lawyers and lobbyists, Anselmo fielded three advocates: Goldberg and Spector, name partners in a D.C. law firm that specialized in telecommunications issues, and Janet R. Studley, a lawyer-lobbyist from the Washington office of Holland & Knight, the largest law firm in Florida. Goldberg had worked on communications issues out of the White House for the Nixon and Ford administrations, and Spector had served two years as an assistant to President Carter. Studley had valuable Hill experience and contacts from her prior position as a top aide to former Florida Senator Lawton Chiles. Anselmo's team not only spoke

THE MOMENT THAT CHANGED THE ENTIRE FUTURE OF BUSINESS AVIATION.

When the wheels of the Citation X first lifted off the runway, corporate travel was changed forever. The fastest business jet in history had taken its maiden flight. And traveling at nearly the speed of sound had become a reality for business. A trip from L.A. to New York was reduced to less than 4 hours. New York to London shrank to 6½ hours.

For years, Citations have made jet speed a practical tool for excelling in business. Now, the Citation X makes it practically supersonic.

THE SENSIBLE CITATIONS

Cessna
A Textron Company

the language of Washington, it knew the communications players inside and outside government.

Anselmo made his first trip to Washington just after his lawyers submitted the petition in July 1990 and met with Alfred Sikes, chairman of the FCC. Sikes indicated the FCC's response would be issued by mid-September, and Anselmo was confident of victory. "The rules that govern international telecommunications were not handed down to us from God like some tablet that came down to Moses," he told *Satellite Communications*. "Who's Intelsat? Just a bunch of phone companies making as many bucks as they can."

But September and most of October passed without a word from the FCC. The delay was the first sign that Anselmo had stirred up something much larger than he was prepared for. Through FCC sources Anselmo's team learned that the State Department had been drawn into the commission's rule-making. Late in October Anselmo's team turned to Democratic Florida Congressman Dante B. Fascell, chairman of the House Foreign Affairs Committee, who had been helpful in securing Reagan's declaration favoring private systems. They wanted Fascell to write a letter to Secretary of State James A. Baker indicating that someone powerful in Congress was watching. Fascell was happy to comply. The foreign-policy ramifications of international communications greatly concerned him. And not only had Anselmo given Fascell campaign contributions, a PanAmSat facility was located in the congressman's district.

Fascell was a potent ally, but unlike Intelsat's allies, he was on the outside looking in. The chairman of the board of Comsat, for example, was Melvin R. Laird, a Wisconsin Republican congressman for 16 years and President Nixon's secretary of Defense from 1969 to 1972. The American head of Intelsat was Dean Burch, a prominent communications lawyer, a past chairman of the FCC, and a counselor to Republican presidents. After becoming Intelsat's director general in 1987, Burch continued to be a key GOP adviser and close friend of George Bush's. Burch's reputation made it difficult for Anselmo to vilify Intelsat. "I like to call Intelsat every bad name there is because they deserve it," said Anselmo, "and with Dean around I couldn't do that." What worried Anselmo most was that Burch would agree that Intelsat had to compete, but only gradually, an arrangement that would stunt PanAmSat's growth.

In addition to Dean Burch, Anselmo had Comsat to contend with. To protect its PSN privilege, Comsat hired lawyers, lobbyists, and consultants that included well-known figures from the Carter and Reagan administrations. As overseer of the operation, Comsat retained Kenneth M. Duberstein, a chief of staff in the Reagan White House and a master lobbyist. Ironically Anselmo had contemplated hiring Duberstein himself while gearing up for the PSN battle; Duberstein would have given Anselmo access to the upper reaches of the administration. But Duberstein wanted a $300,000 fee, and when Anselmo hesitated, Comsat grabbed him.

The FCC responded to PanAmSat's petition by inviting public comment, and Anselmo's team began coaxing letters from supporters such as corporate customers, television networks, telephone companies, trade associations, satellite builders, think tanks, universities, consumer groups, and government agencies. The FCC received 81 comments, only two of which opposed PanAmSat's petition. One opponent was Loral Space Systems, the company that contracted to build the next generation of Intelsat satellites. The other was Comsat.

Next Anselmo's team urged the CEO himself to lobby Washington. "We always encourage clients to come to Washington to plead their cases," said Spector. "People in the agencies or on the Hill are accustomed to seeing me and my ilk. They're accustomed to seeing lawyers acting as lawyers and as mouthpieces for clients. I think it's useful for them to meet the real person on the front line who has the day-to-day problem of making a business go. Unlike many clients, [Rene] didn't need much persuading." From his years with SIN, Anselmo had his own views on how to move the federal government. He believed there "weren't enough human beings in Washington to read all the papers" filed with a typical petition. "I learned then that I should do my own lobbying," said Anselmo. "I wanted [Washington] to know that I wasn't some number out there."

His team set up meetings in early February with a gamut of government entities, from the FCC to Congress to the Commerce and State departments. Some CEOs insist upon meeting only the principal officials and get huffy if they are handed off to a staff member. Not Anselmo. Meetings with a senator or assistant secretary were most desirable, but staff members were more accessible. "It's the staff, the people who do the work, who are the important ones," Anselmo said. "I can be the greatest friend of the biggest political power in town, but if the staff isn't going along, I don't think I am going to go very far."

Anselmo knew his argument had to be crisp and memorable, although to his lawyers' dismay he never prepared. Instead he argued from the heart, exhibiting a fine sense of theatrics. He would sit patiently and respectfully while a politician explained his reasoning, but Anselmo never minced words when his turn came. He was quite capable of pounding a table and shouting "that's b.s." to make a point. "Rene makes his case differently than I would make it as his lawyer," said Phil Spector. "I wouldn't describe him as a consummate salesman. He is anything but slick. I think what he conveys, and what is helpful, is his sense of outrage, and that's very hard for a lawyer in Washington to convey."

Days after Anselmo visited the Hill, letters of support arrived at the FCC from Senators Joseph I. Lieberman, a liberal Connecticut Democrat, and Cornelius "Connie" Mack III, a conservative Florida Republican. But whatever dividends the trip earned were outweighed by unexpected bad news. The departments of Commerce and State announced a 75-day suspension of the FCC rule-making while they reviewed the PSN restriction.

The delay was disturbing enough, but soon Anselmo's team learned that the National Security Council was coordinating the interagency group that would study PanAmSat's petition. Anselmo and his team were old hands at extracting favorable rulings from the FCC. But now the matter was shifting to unfamiliar territory. National security concerns rather than communications policy might decide the ruling. There was a legitimate national security element to the issue. U.S. intelligence agencies routinely intercepted communications transmitted via Comsat-Intelsat. If the PSN restriction was lifted, that would complicate the government's task, although monitoring communications through new satellite systems such as PanAmSat's didn't present an insurmountable technological challenge. Still smarting over the legion of lawyers and lobbyists hired by Comsat and Intelsat, Anselmo suspected the worst: Ken Duberstein had shrouded the issue behind a cloak of national security.

Uncertain what to do, Anselmo's team kept tugging on familiar levers. Janet Studley, who visited the Hill almost daily, pressed sympathetic Congress members to flood the FCC with letters. Anselmo's team provided a sample draft that could be signed and sent with or without editing by a member of Congress.

In April Anselmo returned to Washington to meet with supporters like Dante Fascell and William B. Richardson, a Democratic congressman from New Mexico. Anselmo's team also reached out beyond PanAmSat's usual advocates to Republican Senators Warren B. Rudman of New Hampshire and John C. Danforth of Missouri. As members of the Senate Select Committee on Intelligence, both could find out whether the national security issue was merely a smokescreen.

Anselmo's contacts with these senators illustrate the value of direct meetings. Rudman and Danforth had little reason to be responsive to Anselmo's predicament: PanAmSat had no operations in New Hampshire or Missouri, and Anselmo was not a big donor to the Republican Party. But when the men heard Anselmo describe his investment in the *Bolívar* launch, their eyes widened. Spector, who accompanied Anselmo to a meeting-on-the-run with Danforth, recalled the occasion. It took place "literally in the lobby outside the Senate chambers, and Danforth had a reaction much like Rudman's," said Spector. "The idea that somebody put in $80 million of his own money—essentially cashed out on his life's work and put the money, double or nothing, on a new satellite project—was just shocking." Rudman and Danforth promised to

FLIES LIKE A JET.
BUYS LIKE A TURBOPROP.

From the moment the first CitationJet took flight, the rules were changed forever. Cruising at 437 mph, the CitationJet is the first business jet that significantly outperforms ordinary turboprops at a guaranteed lower operating cost, *and* costs far less to purchase.

The technological advancements engineered into this extraordinary aircraft mean that even with a smaller price tag, the CitationJet has a great number of things the turboprop does not. Including a bright future.

THE SENSIBLE CITATIONS

Cessna
A Textron Company

see whether concerns about national security were legitimate.

Despite such successes, the second trip was a disappointment. A meeting with Commerce Secretary Robert A. Mosbacher had marked the closest approach yet to the president's inner circle of advisers. But Mosbacher would not reveal why the Commerce and State departments had intervened with the FCC ruling. Tight-lipped meetings were becoming a pattern. Normally, key officials share critical information with those who have a stake in the outcome. "They will tell you what the arguments on the other side are or who is raising what arguments," observed Spector. But in this case officials were either inaccessible or mum.

Anselmo returned to Connecticut frustrated and began a letter to George Bush. Realizing that no one, least of all the president, would ever read the complicated letter, he condensed his message into a cartoon. It wasn't the first time he had used the tactic to illustrate a point. Anselmo had penned cartoons previously in letters to President Reagan, the FCC, and Congress members. Those letters of outrage, while widely read, were never published. This time Anselmo wrote a script featuring a quixotic hero and his dog Spot battling an international satellite monopoly and its lobbyists and found a cartoonist to sketch it. He intended to publish the cartoon as an advertisement in *The Washington Post*, *The Wall Street Journal*, and *The New York Times*. Only the *Times* accepted the ad, charging Anselmo $15,000. The *Post* and *Journal* refused to publish the cartoon because in it Spot urinated twice.

Anselmo's team was accustomed to his blunt letters but feared that publishing his cartoon would destroy their efforts to depict PanAmSat as a "company of stature," recalled Anselmo. "Everybody was squeamish [about] a respectable corporate image and all that horseshit. This was the only time I said, 'I don't want a discussion. Lay off.'"

Anselmo's team was dumbstruck by the impact; the cartoon's appearance accomplished more than a dozen soberly reasoned briefs. All anyone in telecommunications could talk about was Anselmo's unusual tactic. The cartoon was "not in the mold of what [politicians] are used to seeing from CEOs," recalled Janet Studley. "CEOs are usually very cautious, but cautious is not a word to describe Rene." Soon the talk shifted from the cartoon to Anselmo's struggle against Comsat and eventually to the PSN issue, the focus Anselmo was after.

Anselmo's team recognized that the cartoon could be its catalyst to a wider audience. The trade press had followed the issue, but the national media could put more heat on the administration. Anselmo's team sought advice from communications consultant Clay T. Whitehead, former director of the U.S. Office of Telecommunications, who managed to interest a *Wall Street Journal* editorial writer in the PSN issue. Two days after Anselmo's cartoon appeared, the *Journal* published a lengthy editorial

Fearing his letter to President Bush would go unread, Rene Anselmo hired a cartoonist to illustrate his script advocating communications reform and in 1991 ran it as an advertisement in The New York Times.

about PanAmSat's predicament, tackling the national security argument head-on. Later that month *Business Week* also wrote a favorable piece.

Washington think tanks represented another way to influence the decision-making process. Following his success with the *Journal*, Whitehead inspired a conservative think tank, the Center for Security Policy, to endorse PanAmSat's position. Altogether PanAmSat helped generate and circulate several think-tank statements to every member and staffer in Congress who had indicated interest as well as to all upper-level officials in the executive agencies.

The publicity from the cartoon made Anselmo think a decision was imminent. But April and then May passed with no word. Even more galling than the delay was the dearth of reliable information about the discussions. Every telephone inquiry yielded the same answer: "No comment." Letters went unanswered. Anselmo assured Defense Department officials that "the proper procedures and mechanisms will be put in place to promote and protect national security." Still he received no response.

Officials were so tight-lipped that Anselmo's team had to guess at possible objections and then respond. "I went to one meeting with a special assistant to [Deputy Secretary of State] Lawrence Eagleburger," recalled Phil Spector. "It was comical. He said, 'I can't tell you anything.' So we would have to say, 'Okay, we understand one of the arguments is X, now here's our response to X. And we understand one of the arguments is Y, and here's our response.' He would just nod and listen. It was all highly classified information, and that made it very frustrating."

Early that summer a Senate staffer phoned Janet Studley and read her a policy paper Comsat was distributing around the Hill. She thought it sounded familiar, so she called one of the few officials involved in the interagency decision-making process who was supporting PanAmSat's position. He told Studley that the Comsat paper was identical to the classified Defense Department memo being used by the government as the basis for the decision. The incident confirmed Anselmo's worst fears. Not only was he being prevented from countering Comsat's arguments, but Comsat was using its access to define the government's position.

Desperate for information, Anselmo's team seized upon a White House press release announcing a new study on telecommunications policy. According to the release, the study would take "a global look at where [the U.S.] telecommunications industry is today and where it could go 15 years from now," with special attention to regulations that might inhibit new technologies. Anselmo and his team began thinking of every string they could pull to arrange a meeting with Vice-President Dan Quayle, whose office would lead the investigation.

Two longstanding friends in Congress, Republican Christopher Shays of Connecticut and Bill Richardson, wrote Quayle asking him to spend

15 minutes with Anselmo. The vice-president's scheduler replied, "Quayle does not meet with CEOs of private companies." A few weeks later *The Washington Post* announced that Quayle was leaving on a five-day trip to Venezuela, Argentina, Brazil, and Haiti to spur private investment in those economies. Accompanying Quayle, the *Post* reported, were Commerce Secretary Mosbacher, financier David Rockefeller, and CEOs from Forbes, Federal Express, Gulfstream, and Comsat. Anselmo concluded that Quayle was avoiding him because of the national security shroud, not because the vice-president declined to meet with individual CEOs.

After one year of secrecy, little surprised Anselmo. The situation was Kafkaesque: key officials were unreachable and the basis for deciding the issue unknowable. "It's very frustrating to have a star-chamber proceeding where all you're told is the result," Henry Goldberg told *Washington Technology*, a trade publication, in August 1991. "You can't go to court. You can't do anything." Lacking information, Anselmo's team relied on rumors. A top congressional aide with some access to intelligence matters told Janet Studley, "All I can tell you is that you have got a problem. Don't give up, though. By the way, this conversation never took place."

It remains unclear whether the national security concerns were legitimate. The intelligence agencies' equity in the PSN issue was undoubtedly considerable, but some sources insist that the shroud that dropped was a sham: it was never a matter of technology but merely a question of expense and inconvenience to the government that Comsat exploited to retard the process. Ultimately, however, even Comsat lobbyist Ken Duberstein's unparalleled access to Washington's top officials could not prevail given the deficiencies in Comsat's argument, the merits of PanAmSat's, and the hard work of Anselmo's team. As Rod D. Chandler, a Republican congressman from Washington, observed in *The Wall Street Journal*, most people have a false impression of Washington lobbying. It isn't "standing in cocktail receptions and patting people on the back," Chandler said. "It's much more a process of making the case." PanAmSat's case, together with pressure from the media, think tanks, and members of Congress— all generated by Anselmo's team—acted like Chinese water torture pressuring the administration to act.

In September 1991, 14 months after Anselmo asked for regulatory relief, the first news of compromise surfaced in the trade press. The Bush administration was going to agree, in principle, to open the PSN to private satellite systems. But they would not have immediate access, and the agencies concerned with national security, such as the CIA and National Security Agency, reportedly wanted a 15- to 20-year delay. Anselmo believed such a postponement would prove fatal to PanAmSat.

Alarmed, Anselmo and his team redoubled their efforts to address national security concerns. They persuaded Democratic Senator Daniel

Inouye of Hawaii to confer with national security adviser Brent Scowcroft concerning PanAmSat's position. Anselmo himself wrote Secretary of Defense Richard Cheney to reiterate his assurance that PanAmSat was sensitive to issues of national security. Finally, Anselmo proposed a compromise: an immediate partial lifting of the PSN restriction followed by the removal of all impediments in 1994. None of these efforts proved successful, however. "We are losing this battle," Studley wrote Bill Richardson in late September.

One month later, on November 27, 1991, the Bush administration issued its decision, seven years after the original determination declaring private satellite systems in the national interest. The administration agreed to eliminate all restrictions on PSN connections by January 1997. In the meantime, private companies like PanAmSat could transmit only telephone calls placed by private networks, such as a corporation's internal phone system, and connect these calls with the broad PSN.

Although not an unconditional victory, it was not Pyrrhic either. Anselmo told *The Washington Post* that the new timetable cut into the "huge competitive advantage" Comsat had enjoyed for so long. "We're happy about [the ruling], but we wish they had ended [restrictions] once and for all." Comsat also claimed to welcome the decision and the resulting competition. "Everyone wins with this decision," said Irving Goldstein, then Comsat's CEO. But a company statement added that Comsat objected to "PanAmSat's underlying goal of utilizing the FCC process and the media for the purpose of 'destabilizing and dismantling Intelsat.'"

If Rene Anselmo had known in July 1990 what his fight would entail, he might never have attempted to lift the PSN restriction. He had anticipated a battle, but only on the merits of business competition, an argument he felt confident of winning. Instead he found himself enmeshed in a petitioner's worst nightmare: not knowing—and not being allowed to know—the arguments and interests arrayed against him.

PanAmSat won against the odds, and much of the credit was due Anselmo. "Without Rene we could not have accomplished what we did," said Phil Spector. "No matter how well known or how effective the lobbyist, he is still just a lobbyist, and everyone knows he's a hired gun. What [a lobbyist] needs is an actual person on the business front lines to come in and tell the story." Of course, without a talented and knowledgeable team even Anselmo would not have been half as effective. Scheduling meetings is relatively easy. But knowing the best people to see is another matter, as is knowing what to ask for. And promises are not likely to be kept unless a CEO has a staff that follows up. As Janet Studley observed, "If you are a CEO from the number-one industry in a state, the promises will be kept. But otherwise a congressional staff doesn't have the time or expertise [to follow up]."

Anselmo harbors no illusions that PanAmSat's future is assured. Having invested time and money to lift restrictions on private systems, he must compete with "free riders," private competitors who waited for Anselmo to clear the obstacles. Nor are Comsat and Intelsat humbled by the loss of monopoly privileges; demand for global telecommunications is growing rapidly. "We're not going to concede any niche in our market to anyone, anywhere in the world," said Irving Goldstein, who became Intelsat's director general in 1992.

To compete effectively, Anselmo must launch three more satellites by 1995, a plan that will require about $425 million. "Rene's pockets are deep," his son-in-law, Fred Landman, told *The New York Times*, "but they're not that deep." So in 1992 Anselmo sold a 50 percent stake in PanAmSat for $200 million. He then turned to the junk-bond market and issued another $440 million worth of securities. The launching of new satellites is only part of Anselmo's two-pronged strategy, however. Anselmo knows that Comsat-Intelsat will try to use the waning years of its monopoly to build an impregnable market position even as PanAmSat advances. PanAmSat aims to isolate Comsat's competitive actions from its monopoly activities to prevent unfair cross-subsidies, demystify Intelsat, and force Comsat-Intelsat to compete on an open world market.

The goal is ambitious; Anselmo must persuade both the executive branch and Congress to take a hard look at the special privileges, including antitrust immunity, accorded to Intelsat and its signatories. Anselmo's team will probably have to add one more lobbyist and a public-relations firm to make Comsat-Intelsat's status an issue. That requires speeches, think-tank seminars, and articles in the press.

Anselmo is prepared to go to Washington to wage new battles, knowing that direct involvement has no substitute. "I think you really have to go down and make your own case," said Anselmo. "I don't see why anybody is going to lift a finger in Washington for somebody they don't know."

The first in what promises to be a long series of skirmishes came in May 1993. Anselmo testified at a House Telecommunications Subcommittee hearing, pounding his theme home once again: under the influence of Intelsat, Comsat, the "monopoly of monopolies," is suppressing competition by using unfair tactics such as hoarding orbital slots. Just in case busy members of Congress failed to grasp his arguments, Anselmo gave Democratic subcommittee chairman Edward J. Markey of Massachusetts a large poster depicting his cartoon dog Spot in a familiar posture: hind leg hiked. The caption read, "Truth and technology will triumph over bullshit and bureaucracy."

IF THERE WERE A CITATION FAMILY REUNION, THE GROUP PHOTO WOULD LOOK LIKE THIS.

When the first Citation was delivered in 1972, its competitors had a big head start. They'd been selling in the same market for nearly a decade.

But buyers know a superior product when they see one. And they began buying Citations. Today, the worldwide Citation fleet has grown to 2,000 and counting. The Citation family has expanded to six models.

And something else keeps growing larger and larger, too. Citation's lead over those competitors who had that big head start.

THE SENSIBLE CITATIONS

Cessna
A Textron Company

Chapter Three

Procuring Inaction

John Young and Rene Anselmo had one broad aim in common: to get the federal government to act. Many CEOs, however, go to Washington to persuade the government not to act. They aren't seeking regulatory relief, federal funds, or the passage of a law. They want to ward off Washington, and although that is easier than prodding the capital into activity, it still requires a CEO's time, effort, and sometimes a considerable financial investment.

With the possible exception of the '80s savings and loan debacle, nothing illustrates the pursuit of inaction better than the minuet between Washington and Wall Street over leveraged buyouts. From 1979 to 1989 LBOs grew until the leveraging of RJR Nabisco, the 19th-largest corporation in America. Washington uttered hardly a word; indeed the Reagan administration hailed buyouts as a natural outcome of its laissez-faire philosophy. Only following the outcry over RJR did Washington begin a brief and ultimately ineffective investigation.

No investment banking firm profited more from this boom than a relatively small Wall Street house called Kohlberg Kravis Roberts & Company (KKR). And no executive was more responsible for the government's inaction than KKR partner Henry R. Kravis. Kravis, a premier buyout artist, went to the capital as a kind of super CEO, the head of a holding-company empire larger than Texaco, Chrysler, or AT&T. By 1989 KKR controlled dozens of leveraged corporations, including RJR Nabisco, Duracell, and Safeway.

1988

HENRY R. KRAVIS
Kohlberg Kravis Roberts & Company

From the mid-1960s to the late '70s, buyouts garnered little attention on Wall Street, Main Street, or on either end of Pennsylvania Avenue. Deals were small and infrequent. But in 1979 KKR engineered the first leveraged buyout of a Fortune 500 company—Houdaille Industries, a manufacturer of industrial products. The Securities and Exchange Commission, which regulates the sale of all publicly owned companies, ordered KKR to produce a diagram illustrating the corporate shells and layers of debt needed to carry the buyout. But the SEC's scrutiny was nothing compared to Wall Street's reaction. For about $1 million, a trio of investment bankers had captured a controlling interest in a corporation boasting $400 million in annual sales. As one investment banker recalled, the SEC documents on the buyout "were grabbed up by every firm on Wall Street. That deal showed everybody what could really be done. We all said, 'Holy mackerel, look at this!'"

The Houdaille deal was even more impressive because Kravis and his partners, Jerome Kohlberg Jr. and George R. Roberts, had been in business for only three years. The men had met at Bear, Stearns in the late 1960s, and in 1976 they formed KKR with $120,000 in capital, most of which was Kohlberg's.

Three years after the Houdaille LBO, William E. Simon, who had been Treasury secretary under President Ford, headed a group that bought out Gibson Greetings, a greeting card manufacturer based in Cincinnati, with an investment of about $1 million. Within two years Gibson Greetings went public and Simon's stake of $330,000 was worth more than $66 million. Taking a public corporation private, paying off the buyout debt, and taking the company public again was yielding profits that had Wall Street scrambling to do the "LBO thing."

As buyouts increased, however, they began to attract unwanted attention from Washington. Buyouts had an Achilles' heel: they hinged on the tax treatment of corporate indebtedness. The IRS did not distinguish between debt incurred from building a new plant and debt resulting from a leveraged buyout. The interest payments on both were tax-deductible. In fact, the higher the interest payments the greater the deduction. This meant leveraged companies like Houdaille paid virtually no corporate income taxes for several years. In some instances the post-buyout deductions were so high the U.S. Treasury owed leveraged companies huge refunds on previously paid taxes. These tax savings, in turn, provided the safety margin of cash needed to pare down the debt. Or as Treasury Secretary Nicholas F. Brady put it in January 1989, "The substitution of interest charges for pretax income is the mill in which the grist of takeover premiums is ground."

Since these tax savings were central to every deal, buyout artists like Henry Kravis wanted to preserve the tax structure. That meant keeping the House Ways and Means and the Senate Finance committees from changing the tax treatment of corporate debt.

As the LBO phenomenon grew in the early '80s, a critic of corporate indebtedness popped up on the Ways and Means Committee—Democrat Byron L. Dorgan, North Dakota's lone representative. As a former state tax commissioner, Dorgan understood earlier than most of his peers that tax considerations fueled LBOs. In 1982 he proposed amendments that would limit the deduction for corporate debt incurred after a buyout or takeover. KKR, along with dozens of other Wall Street firms involved in corporate restructuring, hired lobbyists and tax lawyers to influence the Ways and Means Committee, derailing Dorgan's initiatives.

Aside from the tax structure, Kravis realized his burgeoning industry depended on the laissez-faire economic climate encouraged by the Reagan administration. Indebtedness forced many bloated corporations to become more efficient, and Kravis could point to a number of leveraged companies that seemed better off, including Fred Meyer Inc., an Oregon-based chain of discount stores, Norris Industries, a Los Angeles-based industrial manufacturer, and Golden West Television. But other companies, such as Houdaille Industries, Eaton Leonard Technologies, a California machine-tool company, and the Marley Company, a Kansas construction and manufacturing company, survived indebtedness only by deferring capital investments, slashing work forces, cutting research and development expenditures, or forcing workers to accept wage and benefit concessions. When corporations turned equity into indebtedness, their susceptibility to normal business problems—foreign competition, rising interest rates, and the business cycle—mounted. As John Shad, SEC chairman, observed in 1984, "The more leveraged takeovers and buyouts today, the more bankruptcies tomorrow."

Kravis and others realized that buyouts could be hampered if Democrats won the presidency in '84. Consequently, maintaining a market unfettered by government became as important as preserving the tax deductions. Such a goal required more involvement and commitment. It's one thing to hire lobbyists to keep an eye on the Ways and Means Committee; it's another to try to keep a sympathetic administration in power. In setting such a goal, Kravis joined Wall Street's long tradition of raising hundreds of thousands of dollars for political candidates. Donations seldom buy votes outright, but they can ensure access to busy lawmakers. As former Montana Democratic Senator Mike Mansfield, a 33-year veteran of Washington, once observed, "If a fellow made a big contribution to me during my campaigns and wanted to see me, I'd see him and I'd listen to him. And I'd convince myself that I wouldn't be swayed by his contribution, but deep down [I'd] feel a little obligation."

Kravis was a minor contributor during 1979-80, giving a total of $3,000 to various candidates for the Republican presidential nomination. Over the next two years, as KKR's deals grew, Kravis's contributions grew to $11,000 and expanded to include Republican senators. By the 1984 elections, he had donated $36,000, becoming one of the Republican Party's top contributors.

Reagan's 1984 win didn't mean there was nothing to worry about from Washington. In 1985 Paul Volcker, chairman of the Federal Reserve, vowed to curtail the issue of junk bonds by shell corporations, a key step in the financial engineering of LBOs. "We spend our days issuing debt and retiring equity, both in record volumes," said Volcker, "and then we spend our evenings raising each other's eyebrows with gossip about signs of stress in the financial system." Andrew C. Sigler, CEO of Champion International, spoke for many of his Fortune 500 brethren when he hailed Volcker's proposal. But laissez-faire partisans inside the SEC, the Treasury, and the Justice Department denounced it. Treasury Secretary Donald Regan argued that Volcker would thwart the free market and that if he succeeded he would slam the brakes on a strong economic recovery. Volcker reluctantly backed down, and the way was clear for bigger deals.

In 1986, with an unprecedented injection of junk bonds and scarcely any equity, KKR took the Beatrice food conglomerate private for $6.2 billion. KKR's fee came to $45 million, then the largest transaction fee ever. "I don't think the fees were excessive given the new ground we were breaking," Kravis told *The New York Times*. Size no longer protected a company from a buyout, and the riskier the financial engineering the more enthusiasm a deal seemed to generate on Wall Street. The stock market rose precipitously as investors and arbitrageurs speculated about which corporations were going to be "put into play."

The pace of these events troubled KKR's senior partner, Jerome Kohlberg. After a serious illness he had returned to the firm in 1985, where he found the once sedate business of buyouts transformed. Kravis and Roberts had learned to do without Kohlberg's guidance, and by May 1987 Kohlberg announced his departure from KKR, commenting on "the overpowering greed that pervades our business life." Without ethics, he warned, "we will kill the golden goose."

Buyout fever raged for five more months, until "Black Monday," the biggest one-day plunge in stock-market history. Although the October 1987 crash no doubt resulted from several factors, to Wall Street buyout artists the sole villain was the House Ways and Means Committee. Byron Dorgan had tentatively persuaded Chairman Dan Rostenkowski to propose a $5 million limit on debt-incurred tax deductions. The news of Rostenkowski's backing was enough to prick a speculative bubble. Fearful of blame for Black Monday, Democrats on Ways and Means abruptly backed away from changing the tax code and became snake-bitten. As Democratic New York Congressman Tom Downey explained, "A number of us agreed that [the proposed curbs] were not only bad for the operations of the free market—they were shaking up Wall Street."

With little more than a year to go before another presidential election, Kravis redoubled his efforts to keep the "right people"—politicians who believed in a free market—in office. After Black Monday and with increasing talk about corporate greed, fueled by Kohlberg, Kravis believed the unfettered market was in jeopardy. Opinion polls revealed widespread criticism of Wall Street's financial engineering, and Democrats argued that leveraged deals weakened too many companies.

Kravis's favorite candidate in 1988 was George Bush, who during his

IN SELECTING THE WORLD CHAMPION MIDSIZE JET, THE JUDGES HAVE REACHED A SPLIT DECISION.

Many owners say the Citation VI is the perfect midsize business jet. No other aircraft offers more speed and more stand-up cabin space for less money. Many other owners say the Citation VII is the world's best midsize jet. It's just as spacious as the VI, but it's even more powerful, more versatile, and more technically advanced.

So, is the ideal midsize jet the Citation VI or the Citation VII? Judging by the popularity of the two, we'd say the answer is "yes."

THE SENSIBLE CITATIONS

Cessna
A Textron Company

vice-presidency called Kravis for advice on issues such as "corporate debt and what that meant to the private sector," according to *The Money Machine*, a book about KKR by Sarah Bartlett. Kravis signed on as finance co-chairman for the New York Bush for President campaign, although Kravis knew Bush was not cut from the same free-market cloth as Ronald Reagan. Whereas Reagan Treasury Secretary Donald Regan was a staunch advocate of laissez-faire, Bush's secretary would be Nicholas Brady, a cautious Republican inclined against government intervention but far cozier with corporate chieftains like Andrew Sigler who railed against Kravis.

In December 1987 Kravis hosted a luncheon at Manhattan's Vista Hotel that netted the Bush campaign $550,000. Kravis donated another $12,000 to Bush and $152,000 to an assortment of Republican campaign committees, as well as generous amounts to nine of the 20 members of the Senate Finance Committee. Kravis's wife and KKR colleagues and their wives contributed too, for a total of $418,200. (It was later shown that Kravis exceeded the federal limit on annual donations by $37,000, costing him $8,000 in fines.) The dividend from this support was a candidate more inclined to Kravis's interest than any other Republican or Democrat. There would be no "turning back the clock to the malaise days" of the Carter administration and government overregulation of the markets, George Bush told a Manhattan audience during the campaign.

That October, just weeks before Bush's election, F. Ross Johnson, then CEO of RJR Nabisco, announced he would initiate a management-led leveraged buyout of the company. Ultimately RJR did undergo a $26 billion buyout, the largest ever, but KKR and not Ross Johnson engineered it. At a pivotal moment, KKR turned public opinion against Johnson by leaking details of his bid to the press, including the fact that the CEO stood to gain $100 million. The possibility of such a windfall created a media firestorm, and Johnson loomed as the corporate equivalent of Ivan Boesky, the arbitrageur convicted in 1986 of insider trading. After two months of frenzied bidding, the board turned with relief to an alternative proposed by Henry Kravis.

Although Kravis won RJR Nabisco, influential segments of the business community rebelled against KKR's financial engineering. Two insurance companies, Metropolitan Life and ITT's Hartford Insurance, sued RJR Nabisco because the bidding had turned RJR's gilt-edged bonds into junk bonds. "The value lost by the bondholders will unjustly enrich RJR Nabisco management and other leaders of the leveraged buyout," said John Creedon, CEO of Metropolitan, when the suit was filed. Paul Volcker, who had been largely unsuccessful in his effort to dampen buyout fever, called up Creedon and uttered one word: "Bravo."

Volcker's successor, Alan Greenspan, began urging Congress to explore bank exposure to LBO loans and how those loans might perform in a recession. Congress needed little encouragement to enter the fray. Prodded by headlines and opinion polls, nine House and Senate committees—including the House Ways and Means panel, the Energy and Commerce Committee, known for its thorough investigations, and the Senate Finance Committee—announced hearings on leveraged buyouts, among them the RJR deal. The furor reached such a pitch that President-elect Bush announced at a January 12 press conference that the Treasury Department would review the LBO issue, and if appropriate he would reduce the tax deduction that encouraged corporate indebtedness.

Bush's statement sent shivers through the buyout artists who had invested in his candidacy. Most deal-makers had predicted that with Bush in office no action would be taken despite the public furor. But now they feared Washington might indeed alter the tax provisions that encouraged indebtedness.

Until 1989 Kravis had secured government inaction with little direct lobbying. Besides retaining a law firm to track developments on the Ways and Means Committee, he had financially supported strategically placed politicians. But following the RJR buyout, a different kind of commitment was necessary. If he intended to fight restrictions on LBOs, Kravis would have to counter what he viewed as erroneous charges against buyouts. As he told *Fortune* in late December, "One of the biggest missing ingredients in Congress right now is information and understanding about LBOs. We're prepared to take the necessary time, as are others in the business, to try to increase public understanding of these transactions. Sure there are bad LBOs. But they are only hiccups in the business, the exceptions. KKR hasn't had any like that."

Kravis's initial target, however, was not Congress but the administration, specifically the Treasury Department. If Treasury did not take the lead on such a sensitive tax issue, it was unlikely Congress would. Ways and Means Democrats still shuddered at the memory of being blamed for Black Monday. And Kravis knew his views would be taken seriously within the administration. Not only was he the premier buyout practitioner, but he had helped raise large sums for the Bush campaign. Indeed, as a reward, Kravis had served as co-chairman of the president's inaugural dinner. It seemed unlikely that the administration would take a position at odds with the interests of a major donor, even if, as budget chief Richard Darman told reporters, Secretary Brady privately agreed with Darman that LBOs were "nothing but paper shuffles."

Brady's refusal to meet with Kravis was a measure of the chilly political atmosphere. Instead he handed Kravis off to Robert Glauber, Treasury undersecretary. Still, when it came time for the administration to reveal its position, Kravis's view prevailed. In late January Brady testified before the Ways and Means Committee that although he was uneasy about the substitution of corporate debt for equity, Treasury would do nothing but monitor the LBO situation.

Tepid though it was, the new administration's endorsement of an unfettered market was a victory for Kravis. But the battle was not over. Economist Henry Kaufman, president of the money-management firm Henry Kaufman & Company, and congressional critics like Byron Dorgan continued to predict dire consequences if LBOs went unchecked. After Brady's testimony, Dorgan observed that the administration "believes the marketplace is a temple and they worship at it. It doesn't take anybody with a lot of training to realize what's going on in this country. [LBOs are] bizarre speculation." Despite the administration's position, several congressional committees remained intent on holding public hearings delving into aspects of the buyout business that Kravis preferred to keep private. At worst Congress could pass anti-LBO legislation and challenge Bush to veto a popular measure.

A further complication was that the buyout community was not speaking with one voice. While Merrill Lynch, Goldman Sachs, and the law firm of Skadden, Arps were mounting pro-LBO campaigns that reinforced KKR's efforts, some of Kravis's biggest rivals and knowledgeable critics were also petitioning Washington. Among them was Jerome Kohlberg, who was more alarmed than ever by his former partners' buyout tactics. Theodore J. Forstmann of Forstmann Little & Company, a buyout boutique ranked just behind KKR, was also buttonholing regulators and lawmakers with harsh criticism. Forstmann's rivalry with Kravis was legendary in buyout circles, and he seemed bent on exacting revenge for losing out to Kravis during the bidding war for RJR Nabisco. When Forstmann met with David S. Ruder, John Shad's successor at the SEC, in mid-January, Ruder expected to hear that LBOs were great. Instead Forstmann delivered a stinging indictment of Kravis's financial brinkmanship. And Forstmann was pushing Congress to eliminate the tax deduction for corporate bonds that didn't pay interest in cash, the type Kravis made frequent use of and that had often provided the margin for Kravis to outbid Forstmann. Forstmann steadfastly refused to use these securities, which he called the "fake 'wampum' of 1980s finance."

To ward off Congress Kravis would have to mount a sustained campaign assisted by a first-rate legal or lobbying firm. By early 1989 he had retained the well-connected D.C. law firm of Wunder & Diefenderfer. William M. Diefenderfer III was a former staff director of the Senate Finance Committee under Republican Senator Robert Packwood. Other members of the firm—Michael Forscey, Thomas M. Ryan, and Kenneth S. Levine—had solid contacts with Democrats throughout Congress and were active fundraisers for Independent Action, a political action committee that backed dozens of moderate and liberal members. Forscey had worked for Senator Edward Kennedy on labor issues, Ryan was formerly chief counsel to Michigan Democrat John D. Dingell, chairman of the Energy and Commerce committee, and Levine was a mid-level official in the Carter administration. These lobbyists blanketed the Hill. Key congressional aides who had never heard from KKR before 1989 were suddenly visited regularly by KKR lobbyists and partners.

The lobbyists set about countering any adverse testimony about LBOs. When John W. Dowdle, a retired senior vice-president at RJR Nabisco, testified that interest payments would force RJR to sell assets and/or undertake severe cost-cutting measures, KKR promptly contradicted him. Its spokesman suggested that "a former employee who has had no direct involvement with the company for years" was in no position to pass judgment. Added an RJR spokesman, "If Dowdle is right, then the special committee of the board of directors of RJR and their advisers, Lazard Freres & Company and Dillon, Read & Company, are wrong, KKR and its advisers are wrong, 40-plus of the world's leading banking institutions are wrong, and hundreds of investors who are investing in the debt and equity of the transaction are wrong." (Dowdle's prediction of trouble to come for RJR was proved accurate in 1990, however, when KKR had to give the company an emergency $1.7 billion infusion to prevent its bankruptcy.)

Negating criticism was only part of the strategy. Kravis also had to figure out how to present his case for buyouts before Congress. Because of the RJR deal, KKR faced more congressional queries than any other buyout firm. And Kravis, as the most prominent buyout artist, had invitations to testify before all nine of the committees that had announced hearings—a risky proposition. Committee members might accuse Kravis of acquiring his opulent lifestyle at the expense of blue collar workers and the middle class. While Kravis was an outstanding salesman, he was not known for modesty or patience. Wall Street regulars traded anecdotes about his imperiousness and condescension, qualities that led actor Michael Douglas, Kravis's former classmate at Eaglebrook prep school in Deerfield, Massachusetts, to fashion his *Wall Street* character Gordon Gekko after Kravis. If you testify, KKR lobbyist Ken Levine told Kravis, "you'll be eaten up by the media."

Kravis understood the value of personal meetings with members of Congress, and a CEO who seemed aloof or arrogant could aggravate the situation. So Kravis decided to make himself available to influential members in private. Kravis was confident of his power of persuasion. "Nobody can tell the story as well as we can," he told a *New York Times* reporter. And Kravis believed he had a good story to tell: LBOs did not cause economic upheaval but the reverse. Buyouts were a financial solution to "suffocating and gridlocked corporate bureaucracies that were dragging the U.S. economy down the drain." They freed business from "the paralyzing clutches of hidebound corporate bureaucracies."

One of the first and most important meetings was a closed-door breakfast in Washington with members of the House Ways and Means Committee. Chairman Rostenkowski held these meetings to allow committee members to discuss proposed changes in the tax code with the people who would be directly affected. In this instance, Rostenkowski wanted Kravis to make his presentation at the same meeting as Forstmann. But to avoid an unseemly debate, Kravis held out for a separate meeting, where he and KKR partner George Roberts laid out their argument without interruption. Citing successful KKR buyouts like Fred Meyer, Beatrice, and Safeway, they argued that the discipline of debt revitalized corporations, forcing management to prune excess and bureaucracy, thus strengthening the economy.

Then Kravis broached the subject of corporate extravagance, saying that the executives of many debt-ridden companies had grown accustomed to using their fleets of jets as playthings. Among KKR's first acts following a buyout, Kravis claimed, was to ground those planes. Byron Dorgan, familiar with Kravis's lifestyle, interrupted Kravis to ask, "How did you get down here?" When Kravis replied, "We flew down in one of our planes," members chuckled. "But that's different," Kravis protested. "We own our jets."

Most of Kravis's meetings went more smoothly. A key reason was a KKR study prepared by its accounting firm, Deloitte Haskins & Sells. The SEC and the House Subcommittee on Telecommunications and Finance both had requested KKR and other buyout firms to provide confidential information about the effect of LBOs on employment, capital spending, and tax revenues. Kravis realized that by going one step further than the subcommittee's request he might improve congressional understanding. He was accustomed to going into business meetings loaded with financial information and believed the same tactic would work with members of Congress. So KKR asked Emil M. Sunley, Deloitte's director of tax analysis and a former Treasury deputy assistant secretary, to fashion KKR's response.

Deloitte's white paper purported to show what happened to KKR-controlled companies after they were leveraged so that Congress could judge the results for itself. The paper's survey of 17 KKR buyouts found that every company flourished after being taken private. It said that the number of employees grew from 276,000 to 313,000, and capital spending on new plants and equipment increased 14 percent. Despite charges of a decline in R&D spending and product development, the companies spent 15 percent more on these items. Finally, the white paper contended that KKR's buyouts resulted in a $2 billion tax bonus for the U.S.

IN OUR QUEST TO BUILD THE FINEST LIGHT JET IN THE WORLD, WE CONFESS THAT WE CHEATED.

We had an unfair advantage when we made the Citation V *Ultra* the best all-round aircraft in its class. We began with what was *already* the world leader. Every year since the Citation V was introduced, it has dominated industry sales, routinely outselling its nearest competitor by nearly four to one.

Now, with greater payload, range, speed and advanced instrumentation, the *Ultra* pushes this pre-eminence to an entirely new level. At Cessna, we didn't ask ourselves, "Why tamper with success?" We said, "Why not."

THE SENSIBLE CITATIONS

Cessna
A Textron Company

Treasury because capital-gains taxes outweighed any loss of revenue from reduced corporate tax payments.

Kravis was determined to present the study to every congressional member who could decide the fate of leveraged buyouts. And in most instances Kravis made an excellent impression. He certainly didn't appear to be the ogre depicted in some press accounts nor as dangerous as some critics from the buyout industry indicated. Kravis had a knack for walking into a meeting and striking the perfect note of urbanity, briskness, and confidence. The same characteristics that had won KKR the allegiance of countless pension fund managers, bankers, and corporate executives were now brought to bear on lawmakers. As Democratic Congressman Charles E. Schumer of New York commented, "He doesn't come off as a robber baron. He comes off as a nice, courtly gentleman."

During the winter of 1989, Kravis met with dozens of representatives and more than one-third of the Senate, concentrating on Finance Committee members. He sought out even the most determined opponents, although this tactic sometimes backfired. One such occasion was Kravis's meeting with Terry Sanford, a Democratic senator from North Carolina. Sanford, a former board member of the ITT Corporation, had introduced several bills curbing buyouts after watching indebtedness cripple Carolina textile companies like WestPoint Pepperell and Burlington Industries. "He had a sense that these financiers were marauders from New York," an aide told Sarah Bartlett. Sanford referred to takeovers as the "corporate killing fields," and so his proposals struck at the heart of buyout financing: the deductibility of interest payments. One Senate bill declared interest payments in excess of $5 million nondeductible if the debt-equity ratio of a leveraged company exceeded 3 to 1 and if that ratio was 50 percent greater than the pre-buyout ratio.

The meeting with Sanford was one of the few times Kravis lost his composure. According to Bartlett, Kravis confronted Sanford "demanding that he withdraw the bill." Kravis told Sanford, "You have no idea what you're doing. You don't understand this transaction, the financing." Sanford listened but explained that there was no procedure for withdrawing a bill once it was introduced. "Oh, there must be," Kravis argued. Sanford was taken aback at Kravis's brusqueness, but afterward took great delight in having "put one right between the [takeover king's] eyes."

Still, Kravis swayed far more members than he alienated, and his white paper played a key role. Although Capitol Hill leaned with public opinion toward curbs on LBOs, the report fueled a new uncertainty. If KKR's assertions were true, did buyouts deserve censure? Congress realized that the report, which KKR paid for, was self-serving. But the data and conclusions appeared reliable. There was, however, one curious feature: ordinarily lobbyists with favorable data are eager to share them, but KKR asked members of Congress not to share their copies without permission.

The KKR study didn't turn congressional members or staffers into advocates of buyouts, but it did "muddy the waters" at a crucial time, according to one financial reporter. Flak from constituents about the LBO craziness on Wall Street drove a thirst for information and action on Capitol Hill. The study deflated the anti-LBO movement by blocking political consensus. And KKR's stand emboldened other Wall Street firms, still cowering from bad publicity, to come out in praise of LBOs. The study stemmed the bad press, and with it congressional concern.

Some levers of power, however, remained beyond persuasion. Moved by the same alarms that had prompted Paul Volcker to take action in 1986, Fed chairman Alan Greenspan pressured major banks to reduce their exposure to highly leveraged transactions. There was still no love lost between the Federal Reserve and Kravis. That spring E. Gerald Corrigan, president of the New York Federal Reserve, accepted an award from Columbia Business School's alumni association, noting that the previous year's winner was Henry Kravis. "It raises in my mind a question about your definition of business," Corrigan said, drawing murmurs from the black-tie audience at the Waldorf-Astoria. Corrigan suggested that America needed more mechanical and electrical engineering and less financial engineering.

Kravis's other problem was John Dingell of the Energy and Commerce Committee. Dingell was intent on investigating the RJR deal and would likely subpoena key witnesses. Kravis's critics, such as Jerome Kohlberg, spent hours informing Dingell's investigators about the deal so they could probe its soft spots. Aided by Tom Ryan, one of his Washington lobbyists and a former counsel to Dingell, Kravis walked committee investigators through the RJR deal. Kravis's position was that because of the buyout's size and the fact that RJR was the object of a bidding war, it was a less than representative case study, and the investigators eventually concurred. Consequently, Dingell never held a public hearing because, as one aide put it, "he is not known for putting on empty exercises."

By the spring of 1989, after four months of hard work, Kravis and others had checked the anti-LBO movement. But a new development marred that accomplishment. Two economists, William F. Long, a former Federal Trade Commission economist who was then a guest scholar at the Brookings Institution, and David J. Ravenscraft, an associate professor at the University of North Carolina's business school, were researching the economic effects of LBOs. They got their hands on KKR's white paper, and unlike Congress and the media they examined the data rigorously. The paper's only methodologically sound conclusion, they found, was that LBOs produced high profits for a handful of investors. The claims about greater economic efficiency, higher employment, and increased capital expenditures they deemed specious, based on projected estimates, not actual results.

That May Massachusetts Democrat Ed Markey, chairman of the House Subcommittee on Finance, held one of the last hearings on LBOs in Congress, and half of it was devoted to KKR's apparent sleight of hand. Deloitte's Emil Sunley appeared on behalf of KKR and dismissed criticisms of the white paper as "mostly nits." Markey, however, took exception to that characterization and rebuked Sunley for producing a study whose figures were based on projections and presenting it as verifiable fact. KKR should not have given the subcommittee "quantitative data which cannot withstand critical scrutiny," observed Markey.

Kravis's Washington lobbyists were furious at Markey for holding the hearing. They accused the congressman of grandstanding and excoriated his staff for subjecting KKR's study to such scrutiny. Yet the subcommittee's criticism had come months too late to have any effect on the LBO debate. The political consensus that nothing should be done, shaped in the first place by the dubious study, was now unshakable. Still, KKR paid a price for providing suspect information. No experienced member of Congress expects a petitioner to supply anything but self-serving information. But KKR's study had crossed a line, attempting to parlay a congressional request for information into a questionable defense of the practice of leveraged buyouts that had made Kravis and his associates millionaires. "The credibility of KKR was impeached," said one Hill aide.

Within a few weeks of the hearings, KKR's reputation was further sullied. In August, after months of negotiations, Jerome Kohlberg filed a lawsuit charging that his former partners had enriched themselves by reducing his ownership share in several buyouts. On the heels of this development came more bad news. Three KKR buyouts, including Seaman Furniture and the Jim Walter Corporation, which just months earlier KKR's white paper had touted as great successes, were on the edge of disaster. Seaman and Jim Walter subsequently filed for bankruptcy. Nor could these looming defaults be papered over by releveraging. The junk-bond market was headed for a rout after the indictment of Drexel, Burnham junk-bond king Michael Milken in the spring of 1989, and as Milken's number-one borrowing client, KKR no longer had access to unlimited funds. *The New York Times* headlined its story CRACKS IN HOUSE THAT DEBT BUILT.

To Kravis's adversaries on Capitol Hill, most notably Byron Dorgan, the adverse publicity was serendipitous. "If a good many of these companies begin to fail," Dorgan told *The New York Times*, "those who have been skeptics will have a substantial amount of ammunition to try to slow this [LBO] thing down." Dorgan's initiatives over the years had boiled down to the idea promoted by Ted Forstmann. Forstmann had lobbied the tax-writing committees to limit the interest deduction on non-cash-paying corporate bonds. These bonds accrued tax-deductible interest but did not simultaneously pay it out in cash. Forstmann argued that making these bonds less attractive would slow down buyouts without roiling the markets. The Bush administration cautiously approved the idea.

In the fall of 1989, one year after the leveraging of RJR Nabisco, the limited provision championed by Forstmann became part of the tax code, although it was akin to closing the barn door after the cows were gone. After UAL management failed to leverage United Airlines, the stock market crashed for the second time in as many years. The inability of United to secure the necessary junk financing proved that the party was over. Equity was in and debt was out, at least for the time being.

Henry Kravis's seven-year struggle to maintain an unfettered market illustrates several facets of doing business in Washington. Most clearly it demonstrates the importance of credibility no matter what the goal. Sharing unreliable information is the surest route to ineffectiveness in Washington. Kravis could not hold his own against Ted Forstmann primarily because KKR's assertions lost value after KKR's study backfired.

Kravis's efforts also suggest that procuring inaction in Washington can be just as important as and somewhat easier than securing action. To accomplish change a CEO has to build coalitions. To deflect action, a CEO can use Washington's political climate to help ward off unwanted attention.

Finally, Kravis's case illustrates important aspects of the relationship between money and politics. Kravis has denied having a quid pro quo in mind when he made political donations, but as one political scientist has observed, the special interests that most support an administration also ask the most. Kravis is forthright about his desire for a certain kind of financial environment during the 1980s. As he told Sarah Bartlett, "I have absolutely no agenda on this, and nobody understands this. I want the best person in office, to keep this country competitive and free. I'm very much of a free-market person. I don't want interference."

One irony is that while Kravis significantly slowed congressional action against the buyout phenomenon, he may have unwittingly undermined the candidate he most wanted to keep in office. When the U.S. economy began to slow in 1990, many economists predicted a soft landing, a minor recession before the business cycle perked up again. Corporate indebtedness was perhaps the most fundamental reason an economic recovery has been so long in coming. Taken together, these economic facts killed George Bush's chances for reelection during a campaign that was in many ways a referendum on 1980s-style economics and its chief beneficiaries.

TO ONE CITATION OWNER, THIS LOOKS LIKE PERFECT FLYING WEATHER.

When one University of North Dakota pilot sees a thunderhead like this, he flies directly into it. It's part of his job as a weather researcher. So far, his specially equipped Citation has carried him, his copilot, and a scientist right into the jaws of 600 severe thunderstorms. And right back out again.

It's good to know that Citations can survive rough weather, but it's better to know they don't have to. Citations are built to cruise at altitudes far above most storm clouds. And most weather researchers.

THE SENSIBLE CITATIONS

Cessna
A Textron Company

Chapter Four

THE COINCIDENCE OF PREPARATION AND OPPORTUNITY

For every Henry Kravis intent on stopping legislation, another chief executive is striving to get a law passed. More often than not, he's after a minor legal adjustment such as a federal subsidy or tax break. Sometimes, however, CEOs instigate the passage of fundamental laws that transform an industry.

William T. McCormick Jr., 49, is CEO of CMS Energy, based in Jackson, Michigan. In the mid-1980s, he became convinced that outmoded federal laws were hampering not only CMS's utility operations but the entire electricity-generating industry. In 1987 McCormick began a campaign for reform that five years later yielded the most sweeping overhaul of energy legislation in 60 years. His victory illustrates the old Washington saying that major legislation results from the coincidence of preparation and opportunity. But his odyssey has a sobering side too; it demonstrates the complications and pitfalls that can beset a CEO who achieves a high profile in Washington.

McCormick's prominent role stemmed from his "can-do" personality and his considerable experience in the capital. An MIT-trained nuclear engineer, his first job was to analyze weapons and energy policy for the Nixon White House. He worked for various executive agencies from 1973 to 1976 before becoming the top Washington lobbyist for the American Gas Association. After two years, McCormick joined the American Natural Resources Company as a vice-president and at 39 became CEO. In 1985, five months after ANR was sold to the Coastal Corporation,

WILLIAM T. McCORMICK JR.
CEO, CMS Energy Corporation

McCormick took the top job at Consumers Power Company, a nearly insolvent privately owned utility. Once a premier company, Consumers Power provided electricity and natural-gas service to almost two-thirds of Michigan's nine million residents.

McCormick first reorganized Consumers Power as the subsidiary of a new parent company, CMS Energy Corporation. He then attacked the company's problems. Consumers had a deteriorating balance sheet, sour relationships with the governor, legislature, and state public utility commission, strained ties to some of its biggest customers such as Dow Chemical, and poor media and public relations—all because of one $4.1 billion white elephant. In 1970 Consumers had begun construction of a nuclear power plant in Midland, Michigan, to meet increased electricity demand. Shoddy workmanship and delays stretched the project out for 14 years. Then, when the plant was almost complete, Consumers discovered that the structure was sinking into the shifting soil.

McCormick responded to the difficulties by cutting costs, soothing big customers, negotiating with state and federal regulators, and devising a formula to reclaim the mothballed Midland plant. In two years he managed its conversion into a gas-burning generator of electricity and steam. Forty-nine percent of the reengineered plant was owned by a new CMS subsidiary and the balance by Dow Chemical and other investors. The Midland Cogeneration Venture plant would sell its steam to Dow and its electricity back to Consumers Power.

The Midland conversion marked the first time a failed nuclear plant had been reengineered to use another fuel. McCormick's boldness earned him a reputation as a miracle worker, applause from CMS stockholders, whose stock price rose more than eightfold from $4 per share, and the enmity of Michigan attorney general Frank J. Kelly. Because of a federal law that encouraged independent energy production, Consumers could charge ratepayers more for the electricity from the Midland plant than it could for electricity from its wholly owned power plants. According to Kelly, this meant that rather than private shareholders, captive ratepayers, who had prevented Consumers' bankruptcy by shelling out $99 million in emergency rate hikes, were paying for Consumers' past mistakes. For nearly six years Kelly sought to overturn the regulatory ruling that permitted Consumers to charge more for Midland-generated electricity. His effort ended in November 1993, when the U.S. Supreme Court turned aside his appeal without comment.

Back in 1987, though, McCormick had his eye on more than a state fight over rates. His early success in turning CMS Energy around convinced him to fight for fundamental reform of federal utility laws. Several overlapping statutes governed the industry, but the basic one, the Public Utilities Holding Company Act (PUHCA), was largely unchanged since its enactment in 1935. PUHCA was a securities law designed to prevent the kind of holding-company utility monopolies that went belly up in the 1920s. They had abused their privileged position by engaging in financial tactics such as stock-watering and subsidizing unprofitable enterprises. Tens of thousands of small investors lost everything on supposedly stable utility stocks. Under PUHCA the Securities and Exchange Commission regulated the corporate organization of businesses that produced electricity, effectively deciding what they could own and where. In return, utilities like Consumers Power were allowed to operate as local monopolies producing a predictable rate of return for their investors. For more than 50 years PUHCA enabled the United States to build one of the world's most reliable and low-cost power industries.

Yet McCormick believed PUHCA was outdated. The technology and economics of electricity generation had changed, but the federal regulatory regime had not kept pace. Energy demand was on the rise, and PUHCA prevented utilities like CMS from responding efficiently. Utilities, for example, could not be the majority owners of independent power plants, a provision that complicated McCormick's effort to rescue the Midland facility. PUHCA also forced utilities like Consumers Power to devise contorted corporate structures if they wanted to invest in other areas. And utility mergers were almost unheard of.

PUHCA erected obstacles to the energy-related business opportunities McCormick saw all around him, some of which promised higher rates of return than the state-regulated Consumers Power could earn. The ambitious CEO wanted to build the country's 13th-largest utility into "the premier diversified electric and gas holding company in the United States." McCormick hoped that by the end of the '90s half of all revenues would come from nonutility but energy-related businesses—no small ambition considering that more than two-thirds of CMS's 1990 earnings came from Consumers Power. Removing the PUHCA straitjacket was vital to his long-term strategy.

McCormick realized that deregulation of the natural gas, telephone, railroad, and airline industries represented a powerful argument for PUHCA reform. Still, overhauling such fundamental legislation would be a monumental task. First he would have to get the utility industry to adopt a position in favor of reform. Congress typically passes basic legislation only with widespread support, and securing industry backing promised to be difficult. Since PUHCA's inception, the utility industry's structure had changed little, despite the turmoil caused by 1970s energy price hikes and the cost overruns of ill-conceived nuclear plants. Unlike McCormick, many utility CEOs were content to run profitable regulated monopolies. Their business decisions were often no riskier than deciding how big the next generating plant ought to be. Any CEO who broached radical change—especially a newcomer like McCormick—was bound to evoke opposition if not hostility. And reform would have to win assent from a Republican administration and both houses in a Democrat-controlled Congress and probably overcome opposition from consumer and environmental groups. The task was, in short, Sisyphean.

Two factors left McCormick undaunted. The first and most important was that the industry was in turmoil. Economic and technological changes such as the proliferation of independent power plants had shaken many assumptions about regulation, generation, and transmission. Second, the political climate favored deregulation. The most influential think tank during the Reagan years, the Heritage Foundation, had called for

PUHCA's repeal in *Mandate for Leadership*, a book widely regarded as the administration's strategic blueprint. And as Martha O. Hesse, head of the Federal Energy Regulatory Commission, explained in a 1987 speech, the commission was exploring nonlegislative ways to encourage competition within the utility industry. McCormick's hard-charging nature and conviction, reinforced by Wall Street accolades over the Midland conversion, made him determined to prevail.

McCormick began his crusade by persuading a gathering of CEOs at the Edison Electric Institute, the industry's most powerful trade association, to form a task force on federal regulation, which McCormick himself chaired. Congress took institute recommendations seriously because its members generated 77 percent of the nation's electric power and served more than 70 percent of the customers. After several months' study the task force recommended that Congress modify "the severe regulation" of PUHCA so that utilities and nonutilities could own independent power plants.

The institute formally adopted the task force's position in late 1987, and McCormick turned his attention to Congress. No one had to school the ebullient CEO in how to make his case on Capitol Hill. From his days as the American Gas Association's chief lobbyist, he knew the key was to be prepared with a simple, credible, and compelling story. Congress members have neither the leisure nor desire to master the particulars. McCormick also knew that to enter a member's office propped up by lobbyists was a mistake. Experienced members can tell the difference between conviction and the prompting of hired representatives.

The first dividends took more than six months to produce. In September 1988 McCormick, appearing on behalf of the institute, testified before the Energy and Power subcommittee chaired by Representative Philip R. Sharp, an Indiana Democrat. The first major congressional hearing on PUHCA in at least a decade placed energy reform on Congress' agenda. But as soon as McCormick finished testifying, protest erupted. Many institute members were outraged when they learned about his appearance before Sharp's subcommittee. Internal task forces and talk were fine, but the prospect of genuine legislation was different. The kind of reform McCormick was touting would, among other things, lead to mergers. And mergers meant that several utility CEOs would lose their jobs.

The utility industry was irrevocably divided over PUHCA reform despite McCormick's efforts to forge a consensus. CEO job security was just the tip of an iceberg. At stake were radically different visions of the industry's future. The stereotypical utility CEO was a low-key engineer content to keep technological change at bay. Many such CEOs feared that deregulation would instigate a downward spiral: after making steep investments in new generating plants and covering costs with higher rates,

HOW MANY TECHNICIANS DOES IT TAKE TO CHANGE A LIGHT BULB?

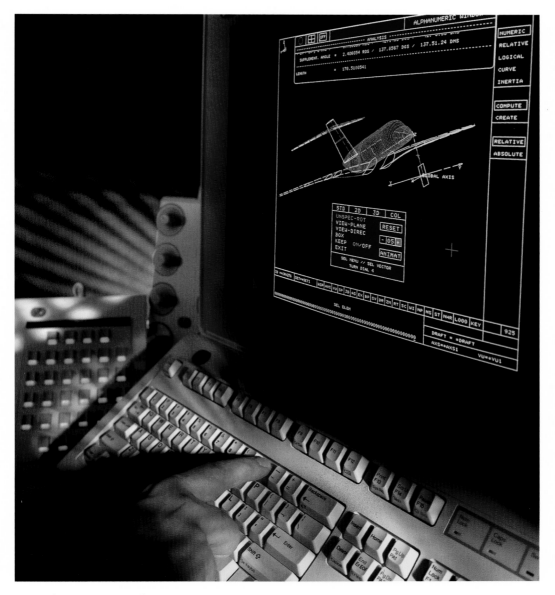

With our Integrated Design program, every concept our engineers develop is evaluated not simply on how it enhances performance, but on how it affects all other aspects of the aircraft. Things like comfort, safety, efficient use of space, and serviceability all go into the equation.

Without this kind of planning, something as simple as changing a fuse or even a light bulb could easily become a complex chore for the aircraft owner. But Integrated Design ensures that no one designing *or operating* a Citation is ever left in the dark.

THE SENSIBLE CITATIONS

Cessna
A Textron Company

utilities would be abandoned by customers seeking cheaper alternatives. That would force the utility to raise rates further, and so the cycle would continue until companies were forced into bankruptcy or merger.

But CEOs like McCormick foresaw a different future. Often recruited from outside the industry to rescue utilities staggering from nuclear plant debacles, these newcomers had less nostalgia for the industry's past. They wanted competition, even if it forced the consolidation of old-line utilities aiming to survive the erosion of their customer base.

Between these two extremes were the undecideds, the majority of utility companies. They were wary of the coming changes but knew resistance was futile. Despite the differences, all the groups recognized that the PUHCA issue was pivotal. If the legislation wasn't overhauled, industry consolidation, as well as the aggressive strategy favored by McCormick, would be stymied.

Consequently, the hearing meant to mark the beginning of a serious legislative process instead revealed the industry's divisions. "A number of members of the institute woke up to this issue," McCormick recalled, "and realized that they didn't support a reform position." The members forced a reconsideration, and ultimately the institute withdrew its endorsement of McCormick's reforms. Split between advocates, opponents, and undecideds, the institute adopted a neutral position in early 1989 and stayed there for the duration of the debate.

McCormick was again in need of a stable industry platform. Within months he had built one, together with eight of the industry's almost 200 other CEOs. The ad hoc organization, called the Utility Working Group, was made up of the largest and best-run energy companies from Virginia to California. Each contributed funds to a central coffer used to hire a Washington lobbyist, distribute briefing papers, and hire a PR firm to blanket the Hill with literature. Not to be outdone, McCormick's opponents, including Michigan's other big utility, Detroit Edison, formed the Electric Reliability Coalition to thwart reform. John E. Lobbia, Detroit Edison's CEO, sharply criticized his peers like McCormick who advocated PUHCA reform under "a phony banner of promoting greater competition and presumably lowering prices." Hill staffers soon dubbed this adamant new coalition the "Just Say No" utilities.

McCormick's individual effort did not diminish with his group's formation. While some other CEOs shared his enthusiasm for reform, none was as comfortable negotiating Washington. "Frankly, back in 1987, 1988, and even into 1989, PUHCA reform was not a big issue on Congress' radar screen," McCormick recalled. "It was not a pressing public-policy issue, members weren't getting any constituent mail on it, and it was somewhat of an arcane subject." The first question members invariably asked McCormick was, "Why should I care about this?" But that bluntness did not dismay McCormick. "Congress is a place where you have to build consensus for action, build a case, and convince people that it's in the public interest to accomplish certain things," observed McCormick. "And it takes a lot of effort to educate members of Congress and their staffs on issues before you can get them to support legislation."

McCormick's top Washington lobbyist, Bernard Schroeder, monitored Congress and provided the information McCormick needed to make his visits count: who the most influential members on this issue were, who was an ally, who an opponent, and who was neutral. McCormick visited Washington, he said, whenever Schroeder felt "that it would be important for me to meet eye-to-eye with the member of Congress or the senior staff person. And I met on occasion with senior staff people, without the congressman, when I felt it was necessary." McCormick estimates he met at least 50 times with members of Congress and their staffs from 1987 to '89, and Schroeder tripled that on his own. Members and staffers could not go to an energy-related function in Washington without running into the CEO of CMS Energy or his representative.

As important as personal visits were, McCormick knew that nothing happened on the Hill without clear communication between staffs. When CMS promised information, it delivered, so congressional staffers readily exchanged information. "CMS Energy's lobbyists always knew what was going on," recalled one staffer.

By the fall of 1989 McCormick had helped create an intense debate over PUHCA and the future of the electric utility industry. The debate, as Washington policy debates often do, involved everyone with an interest in the issue: federal regulators, utility executives, consumer advocates, think tanks, economists, lawyers, and state utility commissioners. Both self-serving and disinterested studies abounded, and PUHCA reform was the subject of countless conferences and intense scrutiny by the energy trade press. But nothing tangible had been achieved since the abortive hearings before Phil Sharp's subcommittee.

To restart the process, McCormick cemented an alliance with Democrat J. Bennett Johnston, chairman of the Senate Energy and Natural Resources Committee. Known for tenacity, Johnston was also a parliamentary virtuoso capable of "mastering the technical details of arcane energy issues, building coalitions to back his approach, and placating his opponents with compromise deals," as the *National Journal*, a weekly Washington magazine, put it. If anyone could get PUHCA reform through Congress, it was the senior senator from Louisiana.

In November 1989 Johnston opened the first Senate hearing on PUHCA reform. McCormick was the lead witness for the hearings, which stretched over two days and encompassed every point of view: CEOs both for and against reform, spokesmen for the Utility Working Group and Energy

Reliability Coalition, and the president of the neutral Edison Electric Institute. Publicly Senator Johnston remained uncommitted. He was there to "learn what the truth [was] on this most important issue," he said. In fact, Johnston believed PUHCA was anachronistic, and his staff arranged the hearing to promote that viewpoint. "We took the extra-ordinary step of moot-courting the witnesses in favor of the legislation," recalled Johnston aide Bill Conway, "meaning that one of my colleagues and I got them in a room and went over their testimony." Johnston wanted a debate, not contending CEOs reading contradictory statements. "It paid off," recalled Conway. "McCormick was a good witness."

On Capitol Hill, when an industry is divided over a bill, there usually won't be one, especially if the issue is complicated. Despite Johnston's support, no vote came in 1989 or '90, although McCormick doggedly enlarged the list of producers and industrial users in favor of reform. Then, in August 1990, the Gulf War turned PUHCA reform into a live issue, reigniting a debate about America's energy needs that had been flagging in Washington since the 1970s. Dependence on oil imports was increasing with little to curb it. Although coal reserves were abundant, burning fossil fuels created environmental problems. Suddenly the burden of proof about any energy issue, including PUHCA, shifted to those who argued in favor of the status quo.

In February 1991, while Coalition planes were bombing Iraqi targets, the Department of Energy announced a national strategy aimed at reducing American dependence on oil imports. Among other provisions, the strategy called for reforming PUHCA to "remove impediments to greater competition." That month Bennett Johnston introduced a 264-page bill that he said addressed America's energy needs. The legislation expanded the class of companies that could generate electric power without SEC involvement. "One of the beauties was that when they started to put together the energy bill everybody was educated about PUHCA reform," McCormick noted. "They understood that it might be desirable, and it got on the table." Preparation had coincided with opportunity.

The legislation marked more than one kind of milestone. At some point every major legislative initiative moves from being an "outside" game played between members and petitioners to becoming an "inside" game of the Senate, House, and staff, one more removed from the private forces that may have inspired the bill. Although the utility industry continued to battle over PUHCA reform, the center of debate was shifting.

Still, McCormick was probably never more engaged in Washington. To congressional staffers he seemed ubiquitous, lobbying at doorsteps, receptions, and fundraisers in tandem or as a tag team with James E. Rogers Jr., the like-minded CEO of Indiana's PSI Resources. In fact, he had become so identified with PUHCA reform that some journalists and people on the Hill nicknamed him the "PUHCA Poster Boy." If you walked around Capitol Hill it seemed as though "he would just pop out of the bushes," recalled one senior staffer.

McCormick's zeal provided an easy target for the *Energy Daily*, a widely read trade newsletter. An April Fools' edition proclaimed that McCormick had had a startling change of heart. "I no longer believe the Public Utility Holding Company Act should be amended," said the contrived McCormick quotation. "Senator Johnston's proposed changes to PUHCA would expose utility ratepayers to unreasonable risks. I will ask my friend Bennett Johnston to abandon his effort to amend PUHCA."

The gag, while amusing, was evidence of an incipient problem for McCormick. He had ruffled many feathers in Michigan with some of his business decisions, including an attempt to shift $1.5 billion in Consumers' assets to CMS to escape the control of regulators and make investments in diversified businesses. Critics also charged that McCormick's cost cutting led Consumers to skimp on maintenance, resulting in annual power outages averaging nearly six hours per customer, triple the company's average from five years before and almost five times Detroit Edison's 1985 total. The hostile climate McCormick inherited at Consumers had not improved, and the relationship between CMS Energy and state officials, especially Frank Kelly, remained tense. Once word of McCormick's high Washington profile seeped back to Michigan, his home-state critics decided to educate Congress about the misdeeds of CMS. McCormick made an effort to settle past and current quarrels, but it came too late. The CEO who helped put PUHCA on the agenda fast became part of the litany of arguments against reform.

McCormick's opponents felt they could turn Donald W. Riegle Jr., a Democratic Michigan senator, into an ally. As a securities statute, PUHCA fell under the purview of the Banking Committee, which Riegle chaired. Riegle had to pay careful attention to McCormick's critics; as one of the "Keating Five," a group of senators investigated for ethics violations after intervening in a federal investigation on behalf of savings and loan profiteer Charles Keating, Riegle was facing a tough fight in the 1994 election and could not afford to be closely identified with Michigan's most controversial CEO.

That September a Banking subcommittee held its own hearings on PUHCA reform. CMS Energy was represented, but for once McCormick was not the spokesman. The hearing was dominated by reform opponents, a coalition of strange bedfellows that included the Just Say No utilities, consumer groups, environmentalists, and publicly owned power companies. These opponents held CMS Energy up as an example of a utility run amok and a precursor to what would happen if Congress loosened PUHCA restraints and permitted other utilities to emulate CMS.

McCormick maximized shareholder profits, his opponents alleged, while shifting potential risks or expenses onto captive ratepayers. If the Senate passed PUHCA reform as McCormick prescribed, the road to abuses would be a paved four-lane highway.

The Just Say No utilities reveled in seeing CMS Energy used to "assassinate" PUHCA reform, as Bill Conway put it. Riegle might have to oppose reform if McCormick's advocacy generated sufficient controversy back home, which in turn might force Bennett Johnston to jettison PUHCA reform to save the rest of his energy bill. That's what almost happened in November, when Johnston brought the legislation to the Senate floor. Riegle and several other Democrats who questioned reform lined up enough votes to prevent final passage. Rather than throw out the objectionable provisions, however, Johnston withdrew the bill.

For two months McCormick's effort hung in the balance. If PUHCA reform could not pass in the Senate, it was unlikely to remain in any final version of the bill, and McCormick's plans for CMS Energy would continue to be strangled by federal regulation. The possibility of defeat was even harder to bear after a court turned down McCormick's effort to use $1.5 billion in Consumers' assets to finance CMS's diversification. The stock market decided, as one Merrill Lynch analyst put it, "it's all over for CMS Energy as a glamorous, exciting, complicated energy venture." CMS stock traded at pedestrian levels after losing half its value in 18 months, and a Merrill Lynch report suggested that a "humbler, more regulatory-friendly management" was in order, rather than McCormick's edge-of-the-envelope style. Late in 1991 CMS Energy did indeed shuffle its top ranks, giving added responsibility for regulatory matters to younger executives who reportedly had better rapport with state officials than McCormick. He remained CEO of CMS Energy but stepped down as head of Consumers Power. The move did little to dampen Consumers' long-running feud with Michigan officials, however. As one former CMS official told *Energy Daily*, "You could make the argument that McCormick is in the wrong job. He's the kind of forward-thinking, hard-charging manager who needs to be out in the real business world where you don't have regulators picking through every little decision you make."

Fortunately for McCormick, Bennett Johnston had internalized PUHCA reform as an aim. Renowned for his ability to compromise while preserving key provisions, Senator Johnston put his stalled legislation back on track. He mollified Riegle by dropping a section that required automakers to produce more fuel-efficient cars. In return Riegle agreed to accept PUHCA reform if affiliate transactions, like Consumers' purchase of electricity from the Midland conversion, continued to be subject to review by state utility commissions. As the *National Journal* put it, the compromise was "a lesson in legislative deal-making, Johnston-style." Concerning

CESSNA HAS INVESTED A QUARTER-BILLION DOLLARS TO KEEP CITATION OPERATORS IN THEIR PLACE.

A Citation's place is in the sky. That's why every Citation is supported by the largest single-product network of any business jet in the world. Today, eight Cessna-owned Citation Service Centers are dedicated entirely to Citations. And Authorized Citation Service Centers are located around the globe. It's a quarter-billion-dollar investment.

We figure the more we spend on the Citation service network, the less time Citation owners will spend on the ground.

THE SENSIBLE CITATIONS

Cessna
A Textron Company

PUHCA, Riegle obtained what amounted to window dressing while gaining concessions on fuel economy that were important to his constituents. Johnston, meanwhile, had kept PUHCA reform in the bill.

Through such compromises, Johnston gathered enough votes to bring his bill to the Senate floor. The Just Say No utilities searched for a new obstructionist, but their unwillingness to compromise made it difficult for them to find a senator to pick up the banner dropped by Riegle. Their heavy-handed tactics did not help matters. The Electric Reliability Coalition favored full-page advertisements proclaiming that another deregulatory scandal was in the making, and the hyperbole angered potential supporters. The coalition had retained Thomas H. Boggs Jr. from Patton, Boggs & Blow, a high-priced D.C. lobbying firm, but even he could not overcome the self-defeating tendencies of his clients. As one of the Patton lobbyists told a Senate aide, if the coalition members "had half a brain, they would accept reality and play to shape the legislation rather than simply oppose it." In February 1992 the omnibus energy bill passed the Senate 94 to 4, with PUHCA reform intact.

Throughout the struggle to get a bill passed by the Senate, the House was working on its own version of energy legislation. The process and politics on the House side were even more complicated because jurisdiction and power were more fragmented. In addition to Phil Sharp's Subcommittee on Energy and Power, the Subcommittee on Telecommunications and Finance, chaired by Massachusetts Democrat Edward J. Markey, had equity in the measure, and any reform had to get by the imperious chairman of the Energy and Commerce Committee, John Dingell. The Michigan Democrat was skeptical about rewriting PUHCA, in part because the original New Deal statute was written by his father, John Dingell Sr., who from 1933 to 1955 represented the same congressional district the son now served. "Unlike some, I do not believe in change simply for the sake of change," he had told a packed luncheon of energy representatives in February 1991. "One side raises the specter of savings and loan type problems if utilities are freed from PUHCA restraints. The other side raises the specter of electricity shortages and higher consumer costs. Both concerns are legitimate."

As the inside game played out in the House, McCormick's role was more circumscribed, although he may not have realized that. House aides describe him as a CEO who didn't know when to quit. "That was a feeling most of the staffers had," recalled one aide. "We know where you stand, Bill, we appreciate your support, we're glad you're on our side, but you're not going to write this bill. He didn't understand that he wasn't in the legislature."

McCormick was anxious about the direction of the House bill. Ed Markey, a liberal Democrat, and Carlos J. Moorhead, a conservative Republican from California, were pushing a provision called mandatory transmission access intended to force big utilities to open their power lines at a profit to independent producers. Conservatives liked transmission access because it seemed intrinsic to a more competitive market for wholesale electricity. Liberals supported it because freer access would reduce demand for new lines, thus lessening the environmental impact of greater electricity production.

McCormick had not bargained for the Markey-Moorhead proposal and considered mandatory access premature at best. Although McCormick espoused competition, mandatory access promised to open utilities to competition from independent producers too quickly. He had been arguing against transmission access for almost as long as he had been pushing PUHCA reform, and it was not part of the Senate's bill. The Markey proposal "needs a lot of modification before it will be acceptable to our company," he told *Energy Daily* in June. "The bill goes way beyond what is necessary in order to assure a level playing field in connection with [PUHCA] reform."

The specter of transmission access further divided McCormick's Utility Working Group as well as the rest of an already fractured utility industry. Nine utility company CEOs, including Jim Rogers, McCormick's peer in Indiana, accepted Markey-Moorhead in a signed letter that made them unpopular among their brethren. Other reform-minded CEOs, including McCormick, believed access was too high a price for PUHCA reform. Meanwhile the bulk of utilities, steadfastly neutral about PUHCA reform, opposed mandatory access. The Just Say No utilities, which were more resistant to change, saw transmission access as an almost religious issue; the House was talking about opening up *their* power lines.

But PUHCA reform without transmission access was, in Washington parlance, a "nonstarter" in the House. And in September, when the Bush administration acquiesced to transmission access in principle, McCormick knew he would have to go along with the Markey-Moorhead provision. McCormick had no intention of being left behind as the Just Say No utilities had been in the Senate. There was still time to modify the provision during the House-Senate conference and ensure that transmission access was "properly constructed and narrow," as McCormick told reporters at CMS's annual Washington press briefing.

In October Phil Sharp converted the Markey-Moorhead bill into an Energy and Power subcommittee document. As the measure moved through the subcommittee, however, an astonishing new provision was attached, aimed directly at CMS Energy. McCormick's critics had inundated John Dingell and his staff with familiar complaints about CMS Energy, including charges that it misused ratepayers' money to finance new ventures, blocked smaller electric companies from gaining access to its transmission grid, and unfairly charged ratepayers more for the power generated by the Midland venture. Dingell responded politically: he instructed Sharp to insert at least one remedy for McCormick's alleged transgressions, a provision that banned affiliate transactions, or "self-dealing" transactions, between a partially owned CMS venture like the Midland plant and a strictly regulated CMS subsidiary like Consumers Power. The rationale was that such dealings were prone to abuse because the bargaining was less than arm's length.

Michigan officials were delighted, and McCormick was speechless. Such a ban would negate a major part of the business freedom he was seeking. He reacted by visiting every member of the Energy and Commerce Committee who would see him, including Dingell. The CEO was at his most persuasive, arguing that in some instances ratepayers benefited from affiliate transactions since affiliates sometimes generated the cheapest electricity. McCormick insisted that it was irrational to prohibit a regulated utility from buying electricity, especially cheaper electricity, from an affiliated company.

Many members privately agreed with McCormick. An outright ban on affiliate transactions was too draconian, and state regulators should be given the flexibility to decide the issue on a case-by-case basis. That was the compromise struck between Riegle and Johnston on the Senate side. But to McCormick's chagrin, his argument created no groundswell to remove the ban from the House bill. Dingell and his staff were convinced that a flat ban was inadvisable. But they did not want to go to conference with the Senate without leverage. Dingell wanted tougher language than the Riegle-Johnston compromise, and a House provision more stringent than theirs gave Dingell more bargaining power. The ban would probably be lifted in exchange for a state-administered regulatory hoop.

Padding a bill is a hoary congressional tradition that makes compromises easier to reach. Such inside maneuvers, however, gave McCormick little solace. On March 11 the House bill—with the ban on affiliate transactions intact—sailed through the Energy and Commerce Committee. Two months later, when the legislation reached the House floor, it passed by a margin almost as lopsided as the one in the Senate, 381 to 37.

Now everyone's attention was on the House-Senate conference committee charged with reconciling the differences between the two 1,000-page bills. McCormick lobbied key legislators hard, not trusting that the ban would get fixed during the horse-trading. The struggle was about more than an objectionable provision; CMS's reputation was at stake. During the negotiations, McCormick pulled off the unimaginable. Through Bernard Schroeder he persuaded his Michigan antagonists—ranging from the attorney general to the CEO of Detroit Edison—to cosign a letter detailing their position on the electric utility provisions, including the ban on affiliate transactions. The letter typified McCormick's understanding of timing and substance when it came to influencing Congress. The state of Michigan and its utility companies had become notorious on both sides of the Hill for their spats. Nothing spoke more powerfully to Congress than to have these discordant petitioners agree on the best form of the legislation. The final version was much to McCormick's liking, especially when a compromise by House and Senate conferees lifted the ban on affiliate transactions—although the transactions would be subject to approval by state public utility commissions.

In October 1992 George Bush signed the legislation that promises to transform the structure of the utility industry and revolutionize the production and consumption of energy in the United States. The president's signature also marked an end to William McCormick's five-year odyssey. When he began, few members cared about reforming PUHCA and fewer still were prepared to push it through Congress. McCormick drove the issue until his basic arguments triumphed. Still, to gain his cherished reforms McCormick had to accept a more competitive market for wholesale electricity sooner than he anticipated. And he had to beat back a punitive measure aimed at his company.

His experience illustrates that Washington is not necessarily akin to a black hole when it comes to fundamental initiatives. True, it will readily absorb a CEO's energy, imagination, and information and may or may not spew out a law in return. If legislation does emanate from the black hole, chances are good it will not resemble the initial request. These twists and turns bewilder CEOs, who look upon Washington, in one senator's phrase, as "a kind of monolithic glob of jello that just can't seem to move." But fundamental change *is* possible.

The business freedom sought by McCormick and his colleagues was manifest within weeks of Bush's signature. Indiana's PSI Resources announced plans to merge with Cincinnati Gas and Electric to form Cinergy Corporation. "Change is sweeping through our industry," said PSI's Jim Rogers, "eventually resulting in fundamental transformation." Several weeks later, Ipalco, a holding company for a rival Indiana utility, announced a hostile offer for PSI. In late August Ipalco withdrew its bid but only after losing a multimillion-dollar battle to place sympathetic directors on PSI's board.

The once collegial and staid utility industry, in which mergers were almost unheard of, will never be the same. As one energy analyst told *The Wall Street Journal*, hostile consolidations promise to be commonplace, because "one way to face this new world is to grab what you can." That this new world exists is due in no small part to the overhaul of utility laws instigated by William McCormick.

IN REAL LIFE, THE HARE BEATS THE TORTOISE EVERY TIME.

For years, the turboprop industry has claimed that slow and steady wins the race. To say that a turboprop is somehow more sensible than a jet is a harebrained notion at best. At nearly 100 mph faster, the Citation II outperforms turboprops in every category, at operating costs guaranteed to be lower. And for virtually the same purchase price.

Today, the turboprop story is little more than a fairy tale. And the time has come, once and for all, to close the book on it.

THE SENSIBLE CITATIONS

Cessna
A Textron Company

Conclusion

The days when an enterprise controlled its own destiny with little government interference are past. As a result, CEOs are petitioning the government in greater numbers and over a wider range of issues than ever before. As Robert H. Malott, CEO of the FMC Corporation, a chemicals manufacturer based in Chicago, observed in Jeffrey Birnbaum's book *The Lobbyists*, "Regardless of how smart you are, regardless of what your products are, you just have to recognize the political process is important. You've got to establish an interface both with public-policy think tanks and those that are responsible in government. You have to come down and establish relationships here; you have to make a contribution. It's part of a CEO's job these days." It's no coincidence that in October 1993 the Business Roundtable, representing 200 CEOs from major corporations, moved to Washington after 20 years in New York.

Washington's receptivity to business petitioners is unmistakable. The city is preoccupied with politics first and governing second. But the fundamental business of Washington is the business of commerce and the economy, and woe to the officeholder who forgets that. The state of the economy is the peacetime standard by which politicians are judged, because the pursuit of material well-being is one of America's distinctive concerns. As James A. Rhodes, the longtime Republican governor of Ohio, liked to say, most elections are decided by "who can put money in people's pockets, you or the other guy." Traditionally Democrats emphasize how workers can benefit from business activity, whereas Republicans extol the roles of owners and management in creating enterprise. But ultimately the promotion of business is a primary task for any successful politician.

Politicians as diverse as George Bush and Bill Clinton have acknowledged this link by cultivating their ties to CEOs. Bush took along 12 chief executives on a January 1992 visit to Japan. And CEOs have clearly been integral to Clinton's politicking and governing. Drawing from a campaign strategy that emphasized corporate endorsements, Clinton consults and deploys CEOs at strategic moments. During the president's January '93 state of the union address, John Sculley, then CEO of Apple Computer, was seated next to Hillary Rodham Clinton as a symbol of corporate support for the president's economic plan. A few months later Clinton inaugurated a series of CEO meetings, conferring with a group that included John H. Bryan Jr. of Sara Lee, Stephen M. Wolf of UAL Corporation, and Harold A. Poling of Ford Motor Company. He lunches several times a month with corporate executives to have "a regular opportunity to hear from business leaders," said a White House spokesman.

For the CEO who accepts this new role, questions remain: How does a CEO effectively pursue his agenda in Washington? Do common lessons emerge from such disparate petitioners as Young, Anselmo, Kravis, and McCormick? It may be most valuable to stand back from the cases and generalize about what works. Some principles:

Washington has its own culture. In the business world, when a CEO decides something should be done, it usually gets done. Not so in Washington. To the outsider Washington is an endless debating society, a place where accomplishing anything is difficult, no matter how sensible or how much a CEO—or president—wants it done. Before Dwight Eisenhower took office in 1953, Harry Truman remarked, "Eisenhower will sit here and he'll say, 'Do this! Do that!' And nothing will happen. Poor Ike—it won't be a bit like the Army. He'll find it very frustrating."

The same holds true for corporate generals going to Washington. A CEO who expects that his desires will be heeded with no questions asked is better off staying home. Every conceivable interest vies for attention in Washington, and the objects of that attention have complex agendas of their own.

Still, a CEO with patience and persistence can negotiate almost anything—even inaction, as Henry Kravis did. Or as John Young showed, a CEO can reeducate the capital. As William McCormick did, a CEO can bring about radical changes in regulations that affect his industry. And a passionate and determined CEO like Rene Anselmo can deconstruct an established monopoly.

Doors are open. Although a CEO from a medium-sized company may not be as well known or have the same backup in Washington as a Fortune 500 chief executive, he can expect a hearing. Officials, especially politicians, like to meet with CEOs, and it's not solely because they expect favors in return. Washington is expert at recognizing power, and business people wield power.

William McCormick and Rene Anselmo demonstrated what can happen when an ebullient or dramatic CEO meets with an eager-to-please member of Congress. Almost as important, McCormick and Anselmo knew that many day-to-day decisions are made by staff and that relations with top aides are crucial. As corporate representative Fruzsina M. Harsanyi put it in *Effective Washington Representation*, "The CEO who refuses to talk to the chief counsel of a Senate committee on the grounds that he will see only a senator is making a mistake."

Some lawmakers prefer not to deal with CEOs unschooled in the ways of Washington. "They're the parsley on the platter of fish," said Democratic Congressman Fortney H. "Pete" Stark of California. "If I have a word of advice to chief executives, it is to stay home and let the pros do it." But Stark holds the minority view. For most members, one CEO who knows how to make his case is worth five Washington lobbyists or lawyers—they're just hired guns who can take any side of any issue. A CEO, who carries the day-to-day responsibility of a business, has more credibility.

It can be time-consuming and disconcerting to negotiate Washington. Most CEOs are used to deference and access, and it's disturbing when a Cabinet member is unavailable or a congressman reveals his ignorance about an important issue. Yet going to Washington is the most effective way for a CEO to get his point across. Congressman Jim Cooper, for example, measures interest in an issue by the rank of those who lobby him. "If a business really cares about an issue, they'll send in their top person," observed Cooper. "And if they don't care about it as much, they'll send in a middleman. And if they really don't care about it much at all, it will be on a list of trade association objectives."

Washington expects to hear from any CEO whose interests are under attack. If Kravis and McCormick had not responded as they did, the legislative outcomes would have been different. As one top aide involved in the energy bill observed, "When there's a harmful provision in a bill, that's CEO material. I think it was very important that McCormick came to Washington. His presence said, 'Yes, I'm concerned. I'm not up in the ivory tower in Michigan, I'm down here.'"

CEOs need translators. CEO involvement is not all that's necessary to accomplish corporate goals. Even the most active CEO needs an experienced translator—a lobbyist, lawyer, or consultant. Washington has its own language and rituals. Besides advice about what's important and whom to see about a given issue, CEOs need translators for follow-through. Without persistence any effort can slither out of control or into oblivion. Each CEO profiled worked closely with people well versed in Washington ways. John Young needed a Tom Uhlman, Rene Anselmo a Phil Spector. Among William McCormick's first acts upon becoming CEO of the ailing Consumers Power was to upgrade the role of his Washington lobbyist. Consumers had had no vice-president of governmental affairs until McCormick appointed Bernard Schroeder. McCormick, recalled Schroeder, decided that "politics were going to be an important part of the company's future, and we had to change the way we were handling our politics because we were getting beat."

Politicians think CEOs who operate without a Washington guide are naive. It's analogous to a lawyer who retains himself as counsel. But not every Washington translator is worth hiring. Many do nothing but meet with their peers without a clue about what is going on inside an agency or in Congress.

An effective Washington representative has to be a presence on Capitol Hill or wherever decisions are made, and his main contacts have to be with executive agencies or Congress. If the translator is not a party to the process, by extension the CEO exerts no influence. Said one congressional aide, "Washington representatives who spend their time in Congress making friends with the staff and the members are very valuable. If you're a CEO, that's the kind of representative you want."

The best representatives gather information, identify issues, provide political context, understand disparate processes, and know who the key actors are and how to get to them. Good translators bridge the cultures of business and government and can influence behavior on both sides. There is a saying among corporate Washington representatives that they spend 50 percent of their time trying to influence Washington and the other half lobbying the companies they represent.

The best help, though, should never be confused with the most expensive. The notion that CEOs must hire a big name is a myth created by those translators who charge the highest fees. "Business is naive about Washington," said Senator David Pryor, "and that's why it pays outlandish, unreasonable fees. I'm amazed that business thinks it has to pay that much." Congressional staffers are frequently dumbstruck by the money businesses spend on big names. Some of the priciest translators do little more than direct their secretaries to make the congressional appointment for the CEO or instruct their assistants to generate reams of memos that go unread. "We laugh a lot about the value not provided," said one aide involved in the energy bill McCormick fought for. "There's no reason to hire a name partner at Skadden, Arps or Covington or Milbank, Tweed at hundreds of dollars an hour. I got a 200-page memo on the interstate commerce clause from Milbank, Tweed. That's dumb." Besides being unnecessarily expensive, hiring a big-name translator does not guarantee success. Comsat did not prevail against PanAmSat despite Ken Duberstein's work. Tommy Boggs did not win the Just Say No utilities a victory against William McCormick.

How does a CEO find effective representation? "The problem," observed Janet Studley, "is that there is so much hype and smoke and mirrors in this business that it's easy to get impressed for the wrong reasons." To win a CEO's business, firms will often make their senior people available. But when the work starts, the big names disappear. It's probably better to recruit someone from a smaller legal or lobbying firm; more important, get references from a trusted source such as another CEO, a member of Congress, or the president of a trade association. Increasingly CEOs are asking firms to submit competitive proposals.

Embrace teamwork and incrementalism. Despite the cacophony of voices, Washington is a team town. Any achievement is the result of teamwork: the CEO has to work for the politician if the politician is going to work for him. That can include everything from writing up an issue brief for a senator or regulator to testifying before a committee. Washington's two-way street requires pooled interests, whether the goal is passing legislation or reinventing the paradigm for business-government relations.

Since teamwork involves compromise, success in Washington is almost always incremental. As Alan Magazine recalled about John Young's experience, "He learned that nobody is going to swallow the whole enchilada. You might get them to take a nibble, and if you do, that's success. Nobody is going to take a report from a presidential commission and implement it—or even half of it. If they take it and say, 'Hey, there are two or three good ideas in here that we're going to run with,' declare a victory."

CEOs who are more interested in results than credit find it easier to win incremental victories. And incremental progress can add up to victory when preparation meets political opportunity. Examine any win and you will probably find it has a long history of setbacks followed by modest gains.

You can't fool Washington more than once. Politics is an exercise in persuasion, and credibility is critical to success. As three-time Cabinet member George Shultz has said, "If you are going to be effective over any period, you have to be straightforward and you have to conduct yourself in a basically honest way so people will have confidence and trust in you." The currency that establishes trust is information. It more than dollars and contacts is the medium of exchange in Washington, because information has the power to persuade.

Government officials initially trust petitioners and their information.

This is especially true for CEOs because of their standing in the business world. If Washington officials insisted on independently verifying all the information they received, they would have time for nothing else. But reliable information is not to be confused with objective information. No one in Washington expects impartiality from CEOs or anyone else.

CEOs who run roughshod over these Washington conventions do so at considerable risk. Nothing is more harmful than being pegged a purveyor of unreliable information. If the best way to nurture access is to have a reputation as a reliable source, the opposite is also true. The major reason William McCormick prevailed despite fierce criticism from his home state was CMS Energy's credibility on Capitol Hill.

Henry Kravis exemplifies the cost of disregarding these conventions. Although Kravis was successful in his encounters with Washington for most of the '80s, KKR's white paper and LBO-related bankruptcies damaged his credibility. None of the members who once took his representations at face value are likely to find Kravis so persuasive again.

Political donations do not guarantee success. Of the four CEOs profiled in this volume, only Henry Kravis made unusually large donations to political campaigns. John Young's contributions totaled little more than $5,000 in the 1991-92 election cycle. William McCormick contributed $20,000 and Rene Anselmo $30,000. The amounts each CEO donated reflect the variety of goals, the degree of opposition, and the focuses of the petitioners.

That all four CEOs achieved their goals despite the differences in the dollar amounts of their contributions suggests no one-to-one correspondence between donations and results in Washington. The nexus between politics and money is seldom as crude and uncomplicated as it's made out to be. More often, large donations simply ensure that a point of view is heard. They create a sense of obligation that's repaid by access. Since politicians often find inaction more appealing than action, large donations can produce resistance to change by chilling initiatives. At the same time, contributions are not foolproof protection against the vagaries of politics. Henry Kravis's friendship and financial support for George Bush, for instance, did not keep Bush's strong endorsement of laissez-faire from turning into merely lukewarm tolerance of buyouts.

Andrew Jacobs Jr., a Democratic congressman from Indiana, tells a story about the CEO of the LTV Aerospace and Defense Corporation who visited him in the 1970s. The CEO wanted Jacobs, then on the Ways and Means Committee, to help him with a tax problem. When he pulled out a check for $1,000, Jacobs said he didn't take corporate donations, but he would introduce an amendment to that year's tax bill that would solve the CEO's problem. "The CEO walked out of the door six feet in the air," recalled Jacobs. "He couldn't believe that someone in Congress would help LTV without wanting a political contribution."

Money is not a politician's sole motive. As Phil Spector observed: "One of Rene Anselmo's big supporters is Congressman Bill Richardson of New Mexico. He's Hispanic and has a great respect for Anselmo for starting this Hispanic broadcasting network. [Yet] there's not been any serious money going to him from Rene. I'm sure there's been some, but it hasn't been a money thing. It's been a personal, passionate commitment."

CEOs who negotiate Washington successfully do not overemphasize political donations. Most CEOs recognize that under the current system financial support is a necessity for elected leaders, and so they donate money to politicians who are responsive to their companies' concerns. Still, most effective CEOs do not rely on contributions except as a limited part of an overall strategy.

Substance sells, style doesn't. In Beverly Hills it may matter whether you prefer Armani to Levi's or veal scaloppine to cheeseburgers, but style is less important on Capitol Hill. More accurately, one style is not preeminent. What all effective CEOs have in common, though, is an ability to make their cases. Washington is responsive to high-quality information. But the information has to be thoughtfully presented, because officials have time to learn only the nub of an issue. CEOs must also make clear how the measures they advocate are important to a broader constituency than their companies. As John Young said, the CEO who is "a narrow advocate gets caught right away. You've got to think through things from a broader point of view."

Most effective CEOs communicate well. Petitioning Washington is similar to making a big sale to a new corporate customer. "It's the same kind of basic skill," said Young. "Find the entry points, track along, look for the window, be credible, be there and get an opportunity."

These lessons constitute the rules of engagement for CEOs seeking to negotiate Washington. And although intended as guides to effectiveness, they are equally important for the myths they dispel. Getting something accomplished in Washington is not, after all, impossible. And you can accomplish your goals without making huge political contributions. As in all business, nothing is as effective as understanding and participating in the processes that get the job done—in this case, the processes that drive Washington.

PETER UEBERROTH SAW HIS NEW CITATION CABIN ON THIS SCREEN FOUR MONTHS BEFORE IT WAS ACTUALLY BUILT.

When entrepreneur Peter Ueberroth came to Cessna to select his new interior, we showed him hundreds of beautiful fabric and hardwood options. Moments later, we showed him something even better – a realistic simulation of his Citation cabin, with all his choices "installed."

This computer visualization system is just one of many surprising innovations at Cessna's new Customer Center. And it's one reason why our owners face no surprises at all when their Citations are completed.

THE SENSIBLE CITATIONS

Cessna
A Textron Company

Additional Copies

To order additional copies of *The CEO Goes to Washington* for friends or colleagues, please write to The Chief Executive Press, Whittle Books, 333 Main St., Knoxville, Tenn. 37902. Please include the recipient's name, mailing address, and, where applicable, title, company name, and type of business.

For a single copy, please enclose a check for $13.95, plus $3.50 shipping and handling, payable to The Chief Executive Press. Discounts are available for orders of 10 or more books. If you wish to order by phone, call 800-284-1956.

Also available, at the same price, are the previous books from The Chief Executive Press:

Getting the Job Done
by Kenneth L. Adelman

What Are You Worth?: The New World of Executive Pay
by Graef S. Crystal

Pressure Points: The Phases of a CEO's Career
by Robert W. Lear

Found Money: Managing the Productivity Revolution
by Al Ehrbar

Who's in Charge?: CEOs and Boards Shuffle Power
by Richard M. Clurman

Getting the Talk Right: The CEO and the Media
by Robert Goldberg

Please allow two weeks for delivery.
Tennessee residents must add 8¼ percent sales tax.